This quote book is the
essence of my 20 years
of reading experience
and I want to dedicate
this quote book to
my 1000+ students,
who came into
my life to inspire
me with their
learning habits
and cheerful thoughts
and feelings they share
with me

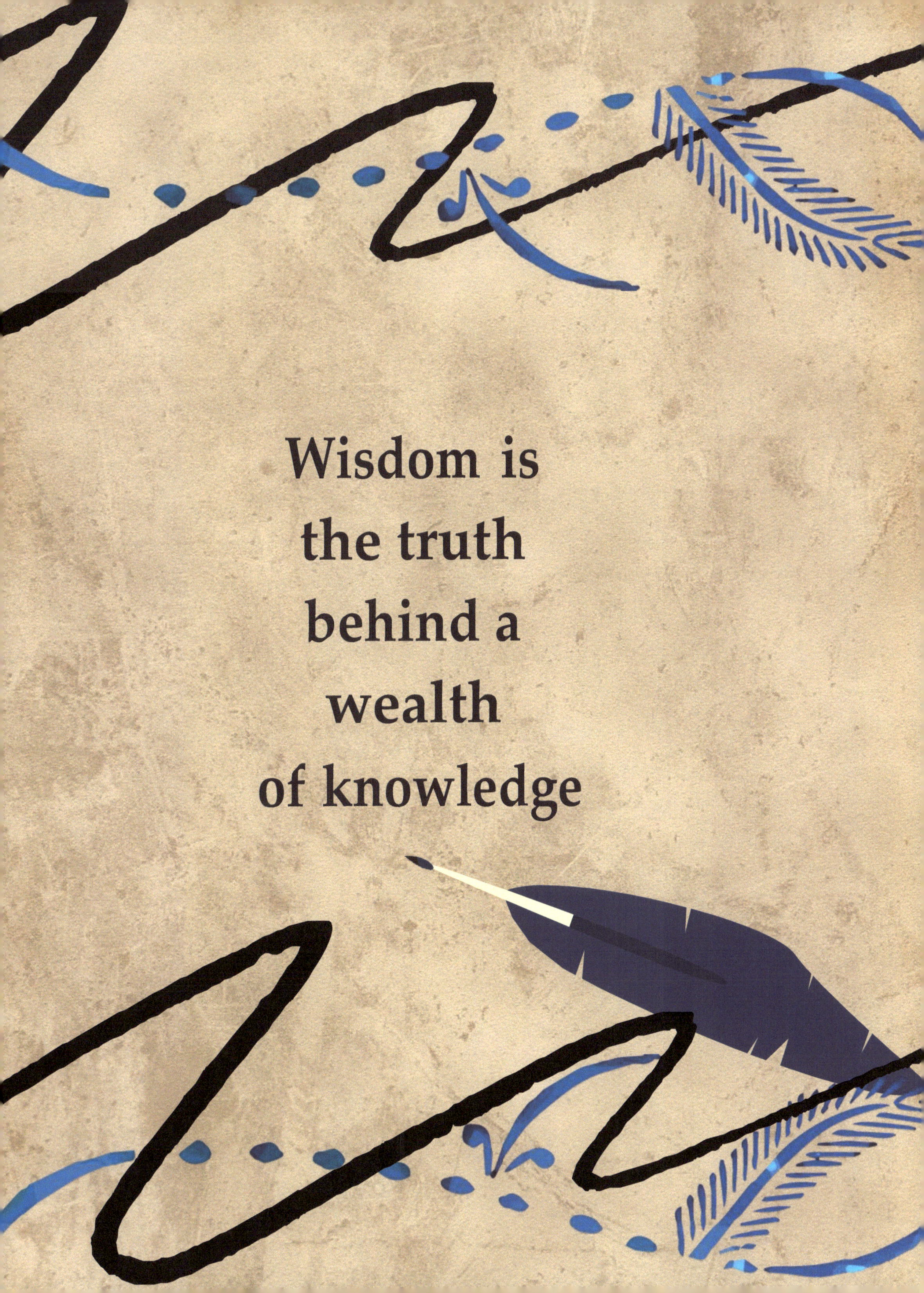

Wisdom is
the truth
behind a
wealth
of knowledge

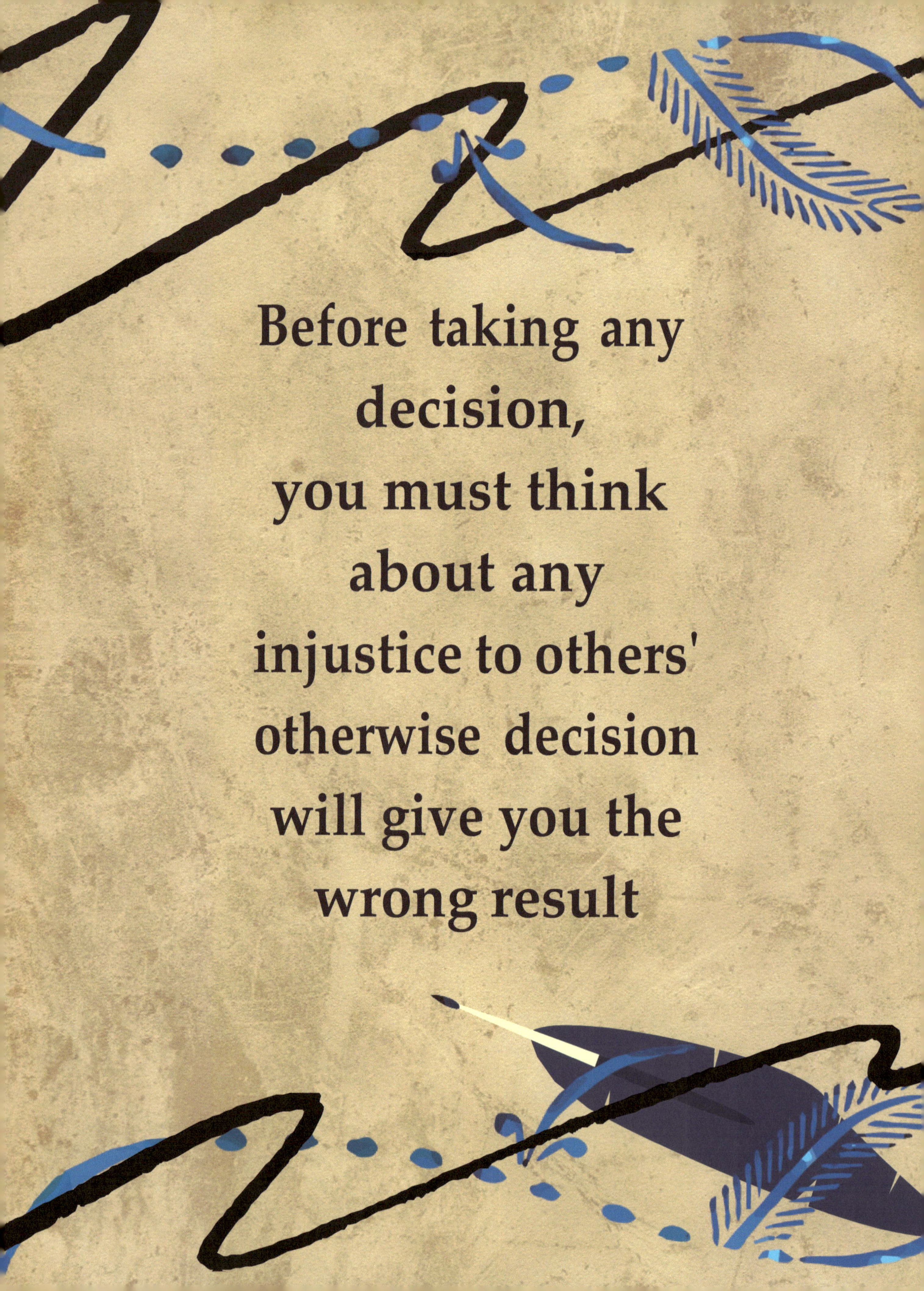

Before taking any
decision,
you must think
about any
injustice to others'
otherwise decision
will give you the
wrong result

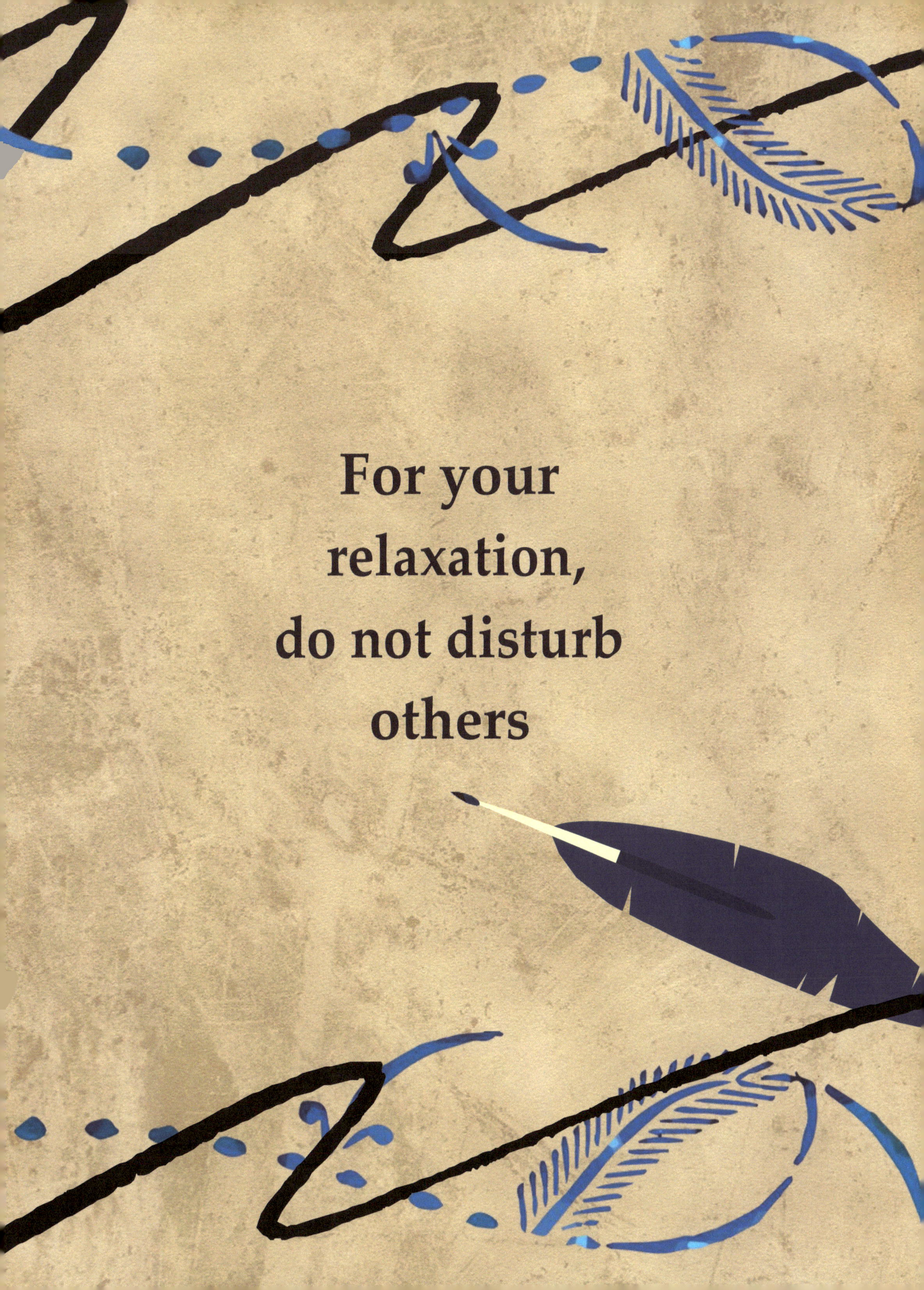
For your
relaxation,
do not disturb
others

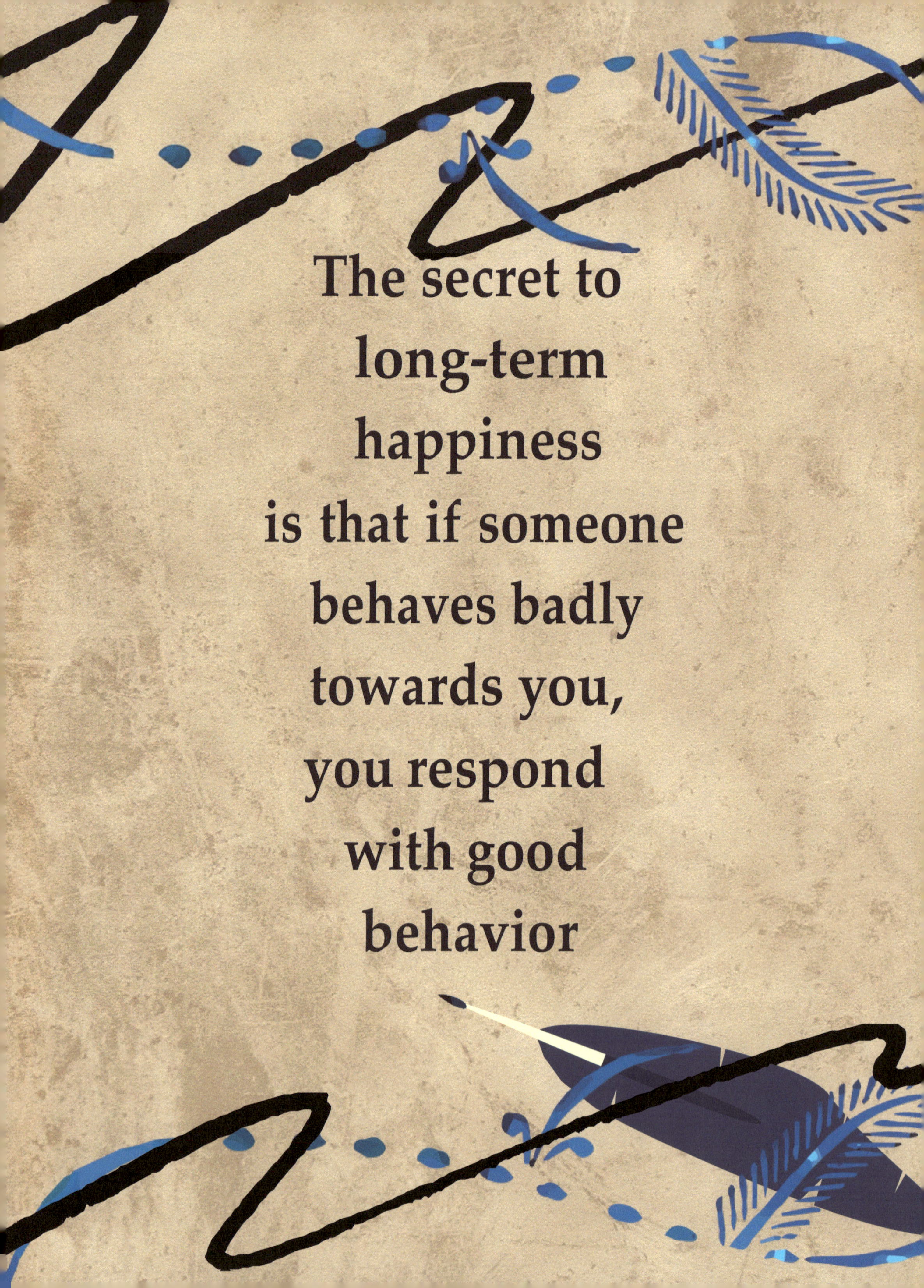

The secret to
long-term
happiness
is that if someone
behaves badly
towards you,
you respond
with good
behavior

Always focus
on
your needs,
not on your
wants

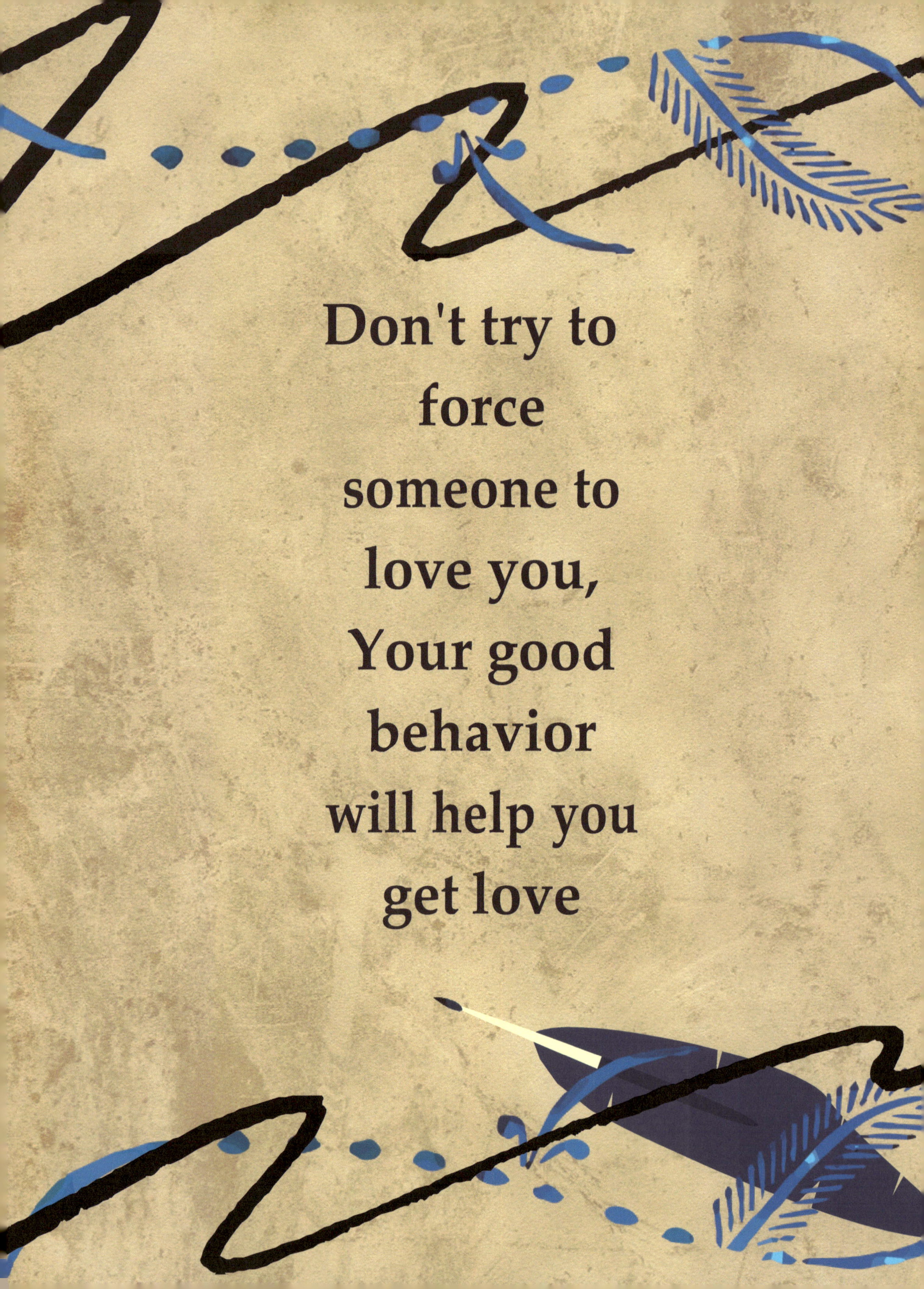

Don't try to
force
someone to
love you,
Your good
behavior
will help you
get love

Your favorite
season is the
season in
which you
are happy

Nature loves all
combinations of
colors because
nature does all
types of
experiments on
color combinations
and they
look awesome

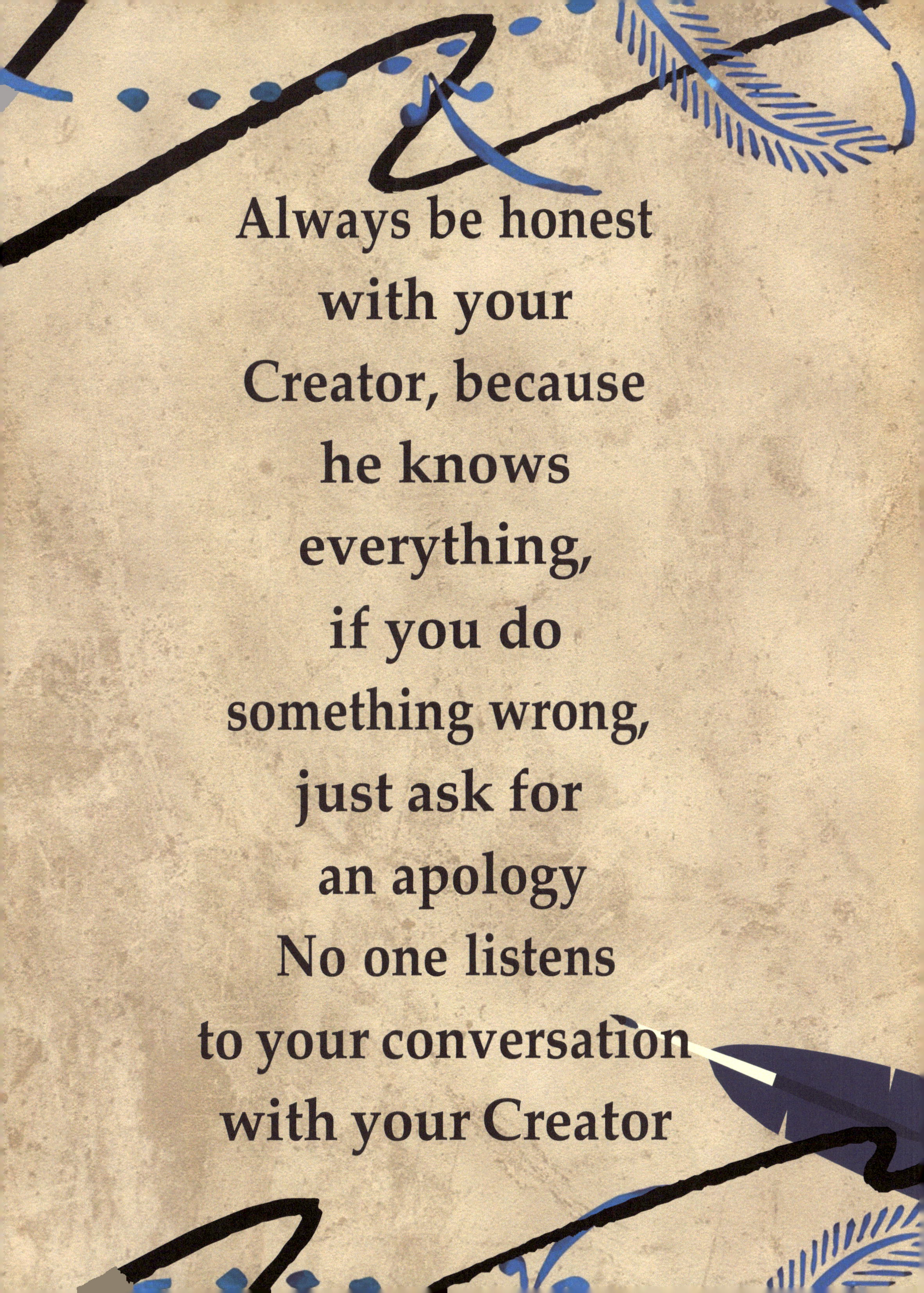
Always be honest
with your
Creator, because
he knows
everything,
if you do
something wrong,
just ask for
an apology
No one listens
to your conversation
with your Creator

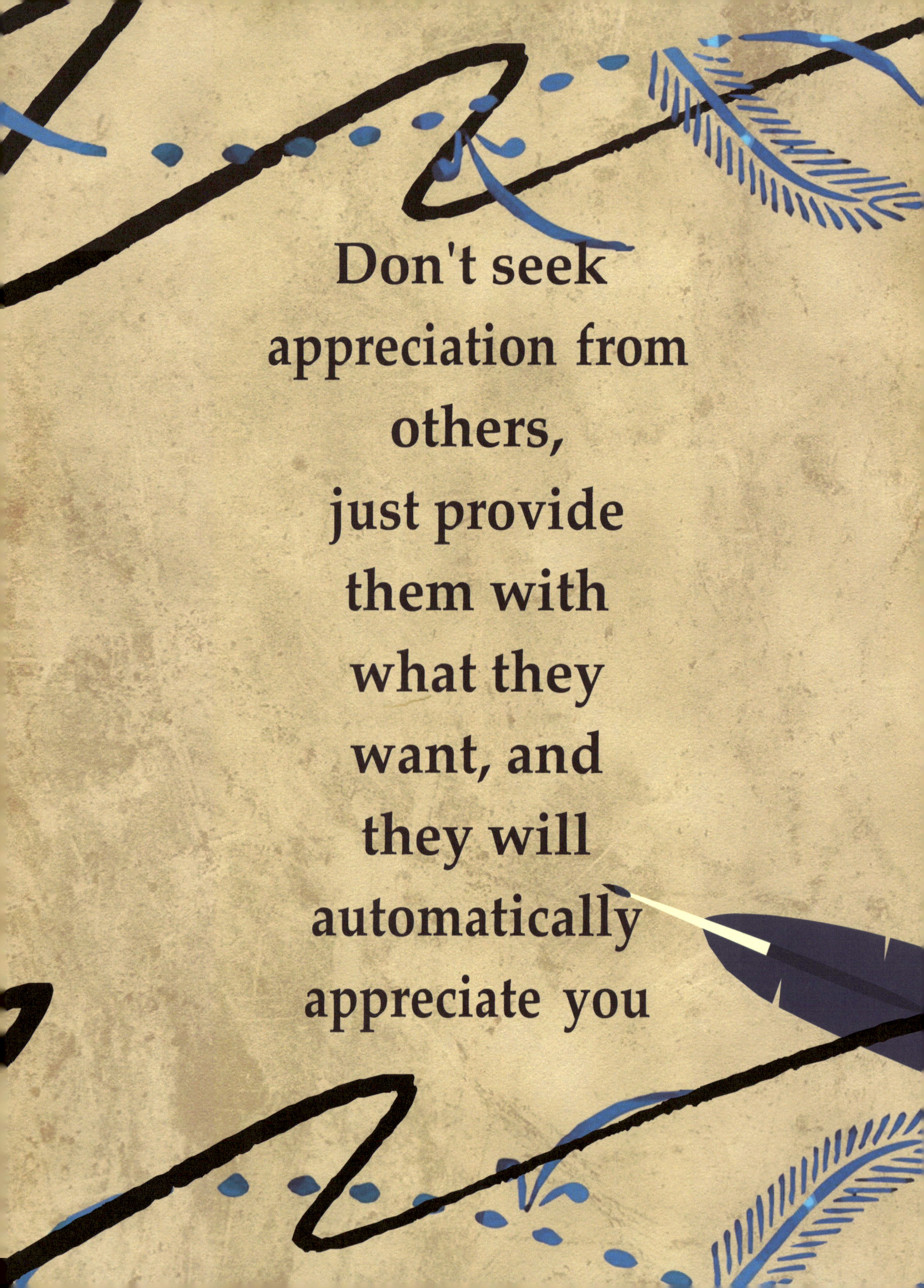
Don't seek
appreciation from
others,
just provide
them with
what they
want, and
they will
automatically
appreciate you

There is a
treasure hidden
in the service
for your parents

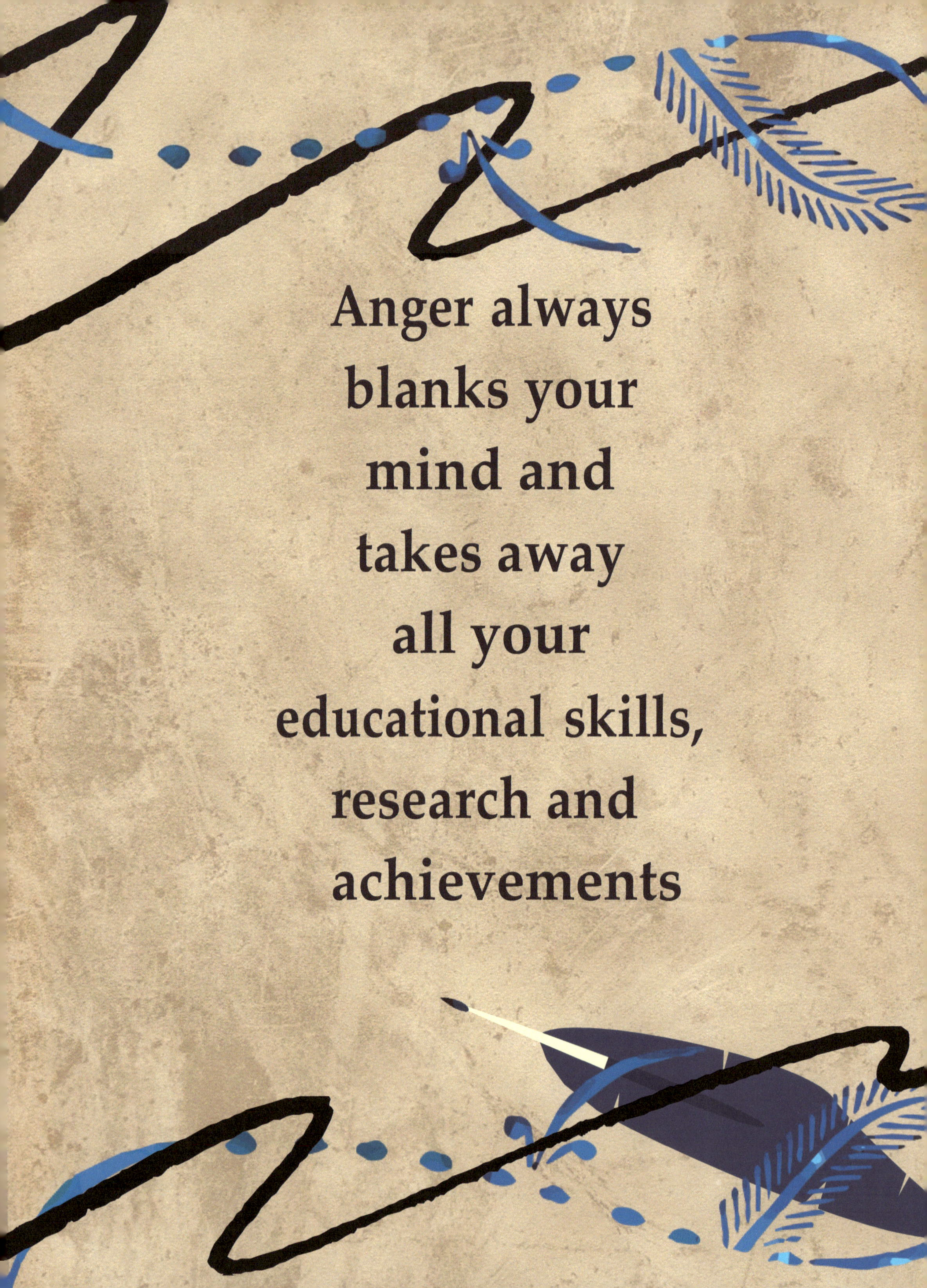

Anger always
blanks your
mind and
takes away
all your
educational skills,
research and
achievements

You appreciate
the work
of nature
through the
careful
consumption
of food
and water

If you want a
deep sleep,
remember your
lucky day

Sometimes,
we just
focus on others'
abilities and
forget our
own hidden
talents

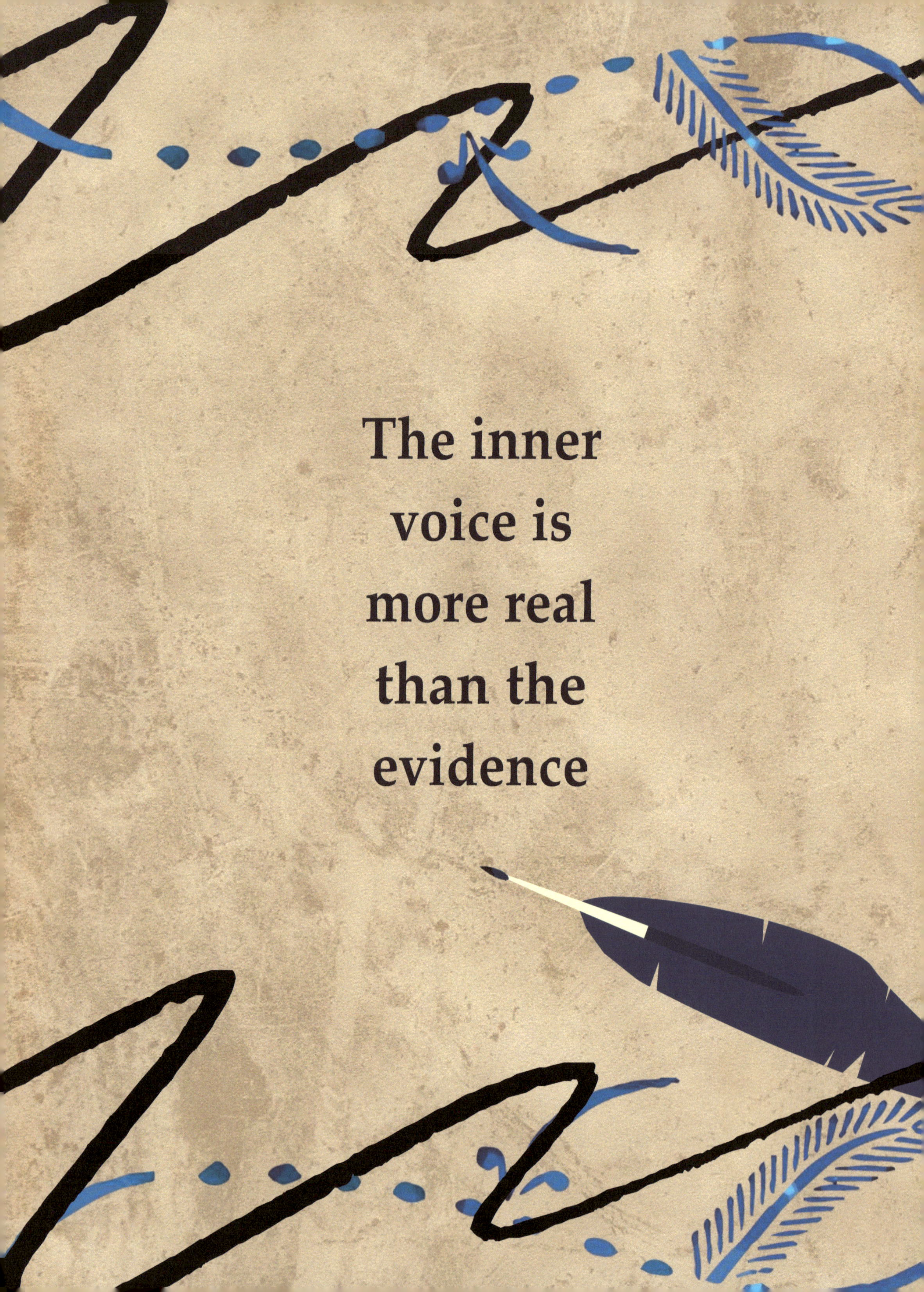
The inner
voice is
more real
than the
evidence

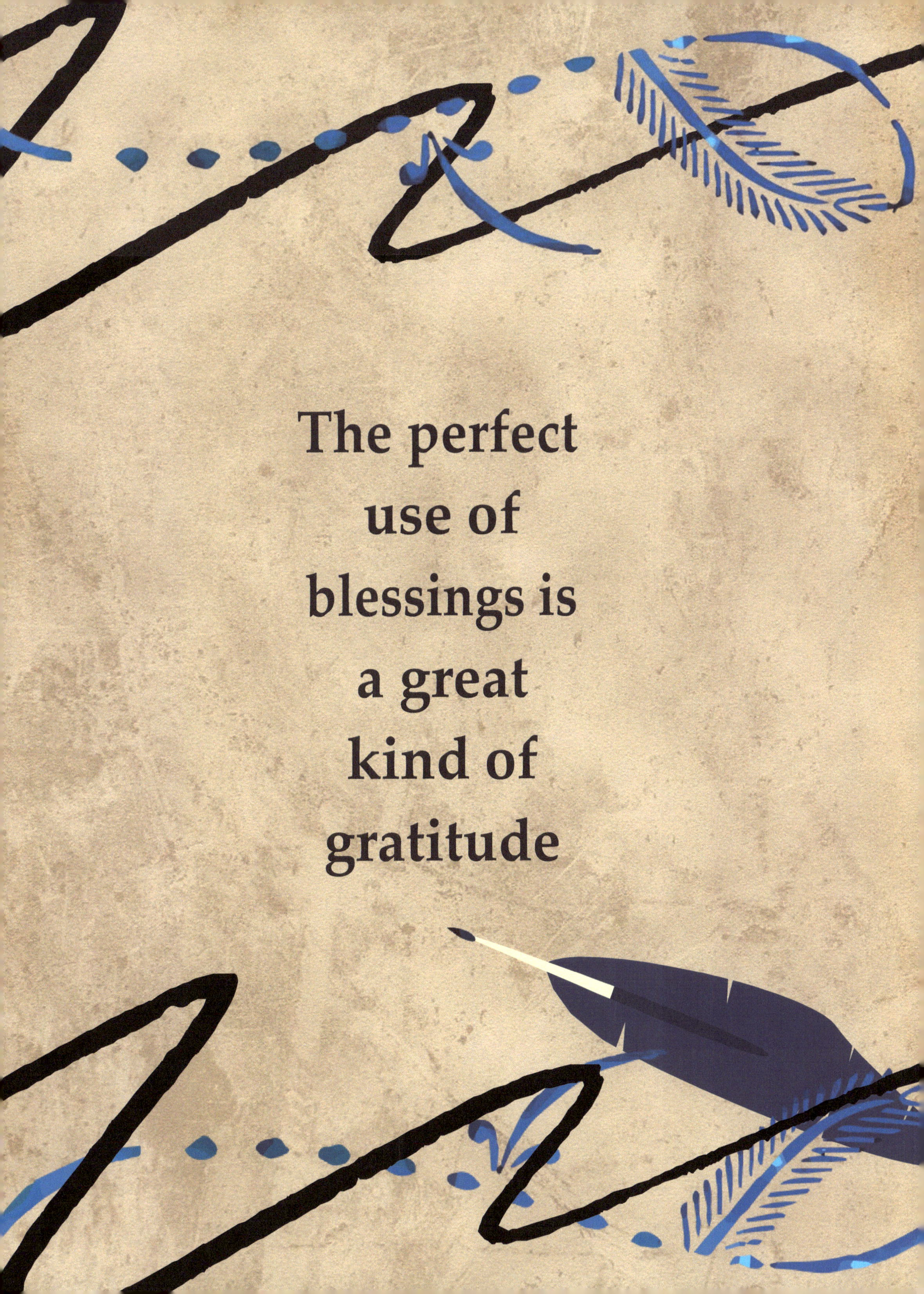

The perfect
use of
blessings is
a great
kind of
gratitude

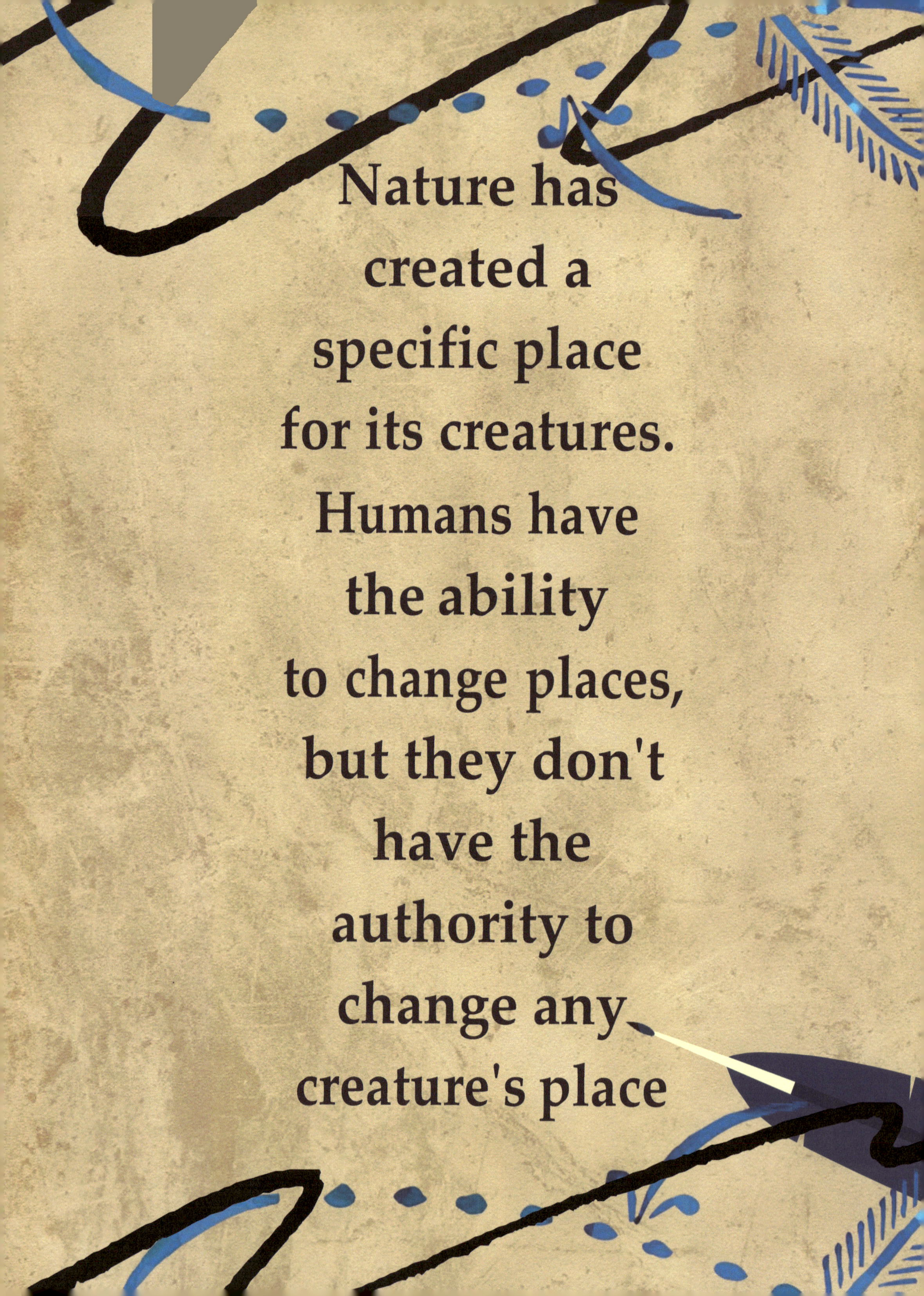

Nature has
created a
specific place
for its creatures.
Humans have
the ability
to change places,
but they don't
have the
authority to
change any
creature's place

Fear is just
our
misperception

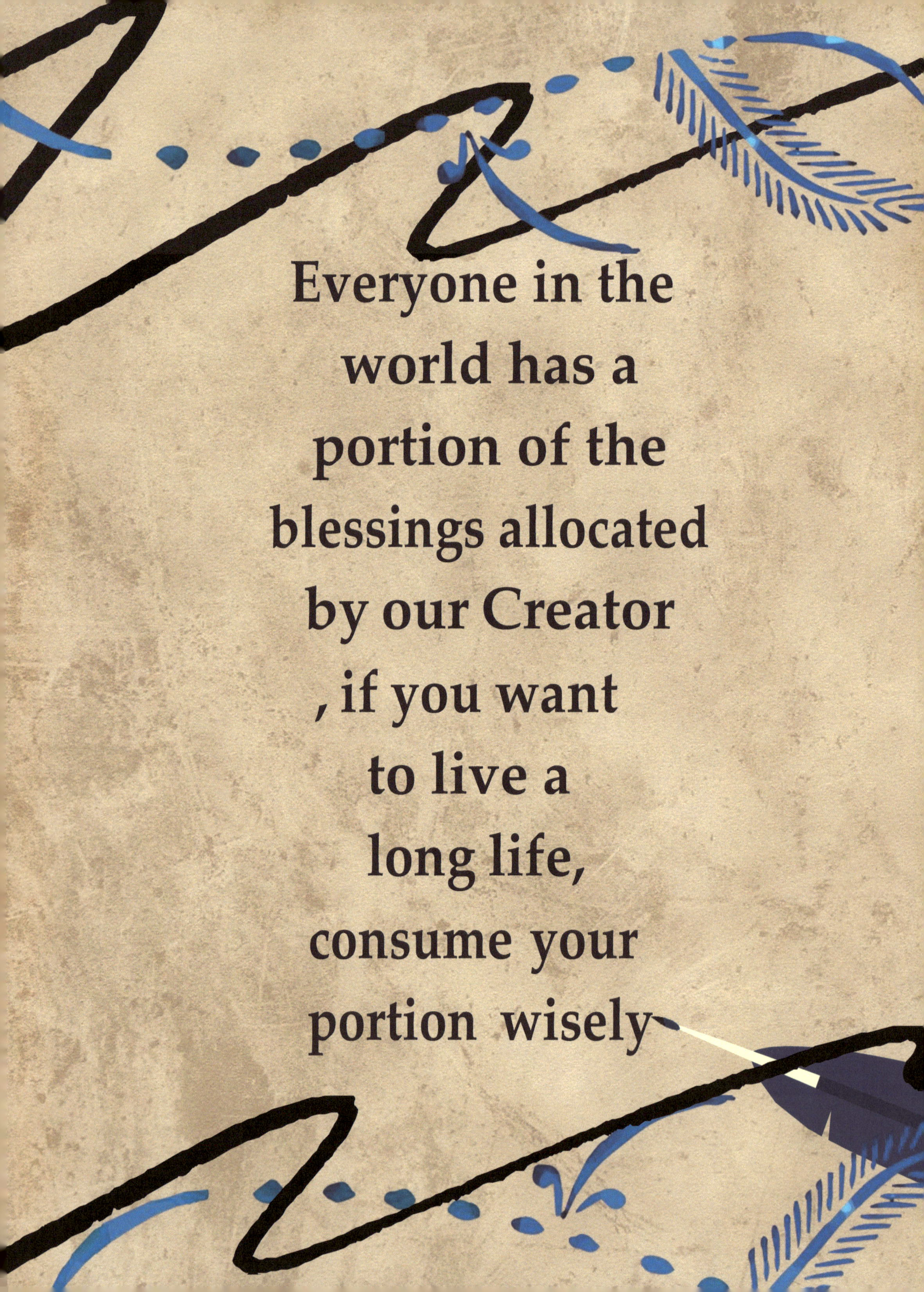

Everyone in the world has a portion of the blessings allocated by our Creator , if you want to live a long life, consume your portion wisely

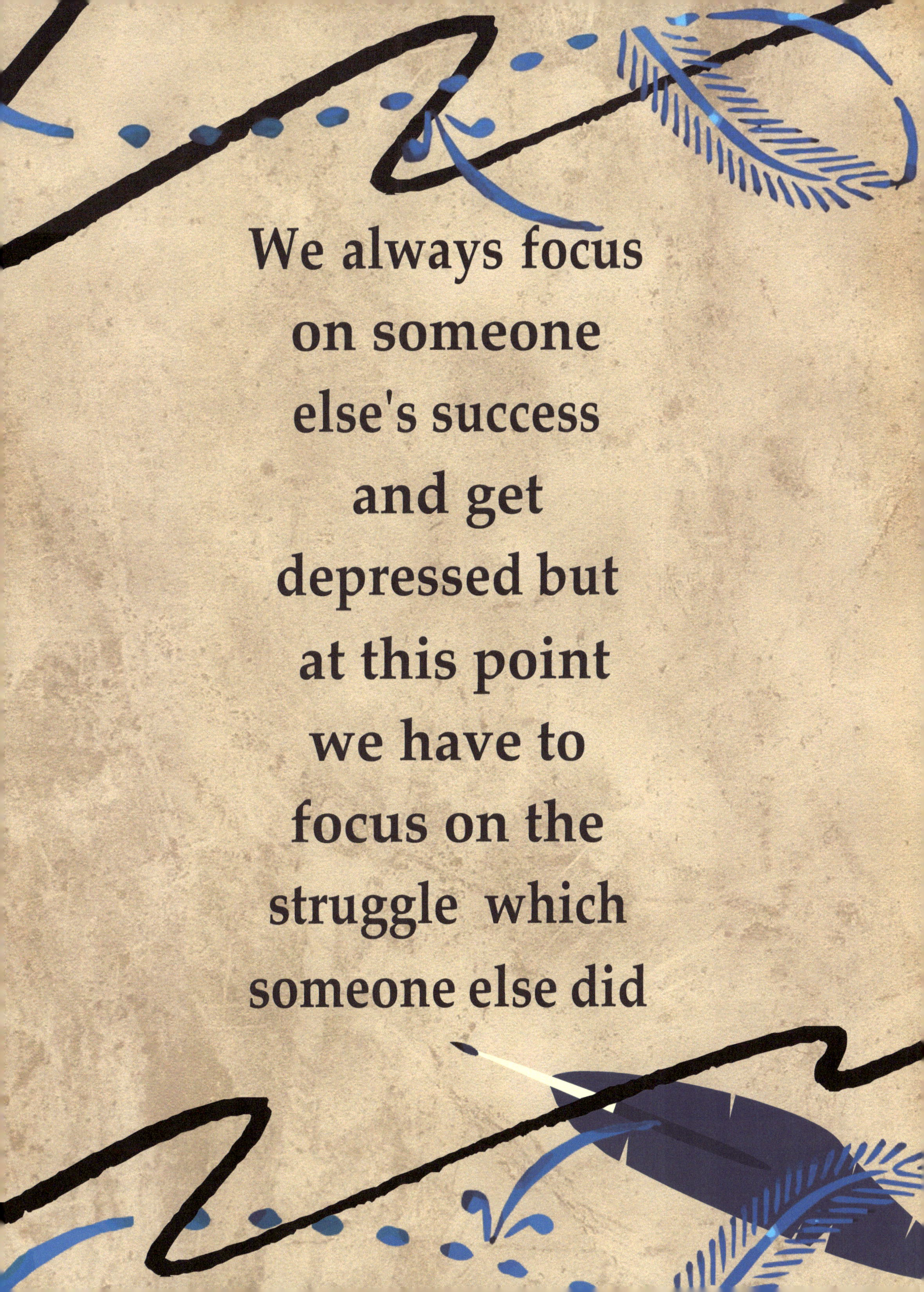

We always focus
on someone
else's success
and get
depressed but
at this point
we have to
focus on the
struggle which
someone else did

Don't make
friends
with the
intention
of helping
in the future

Real help is when
you explain
to your friend
the real cause
of the problem
so he can
realize it
and fix it

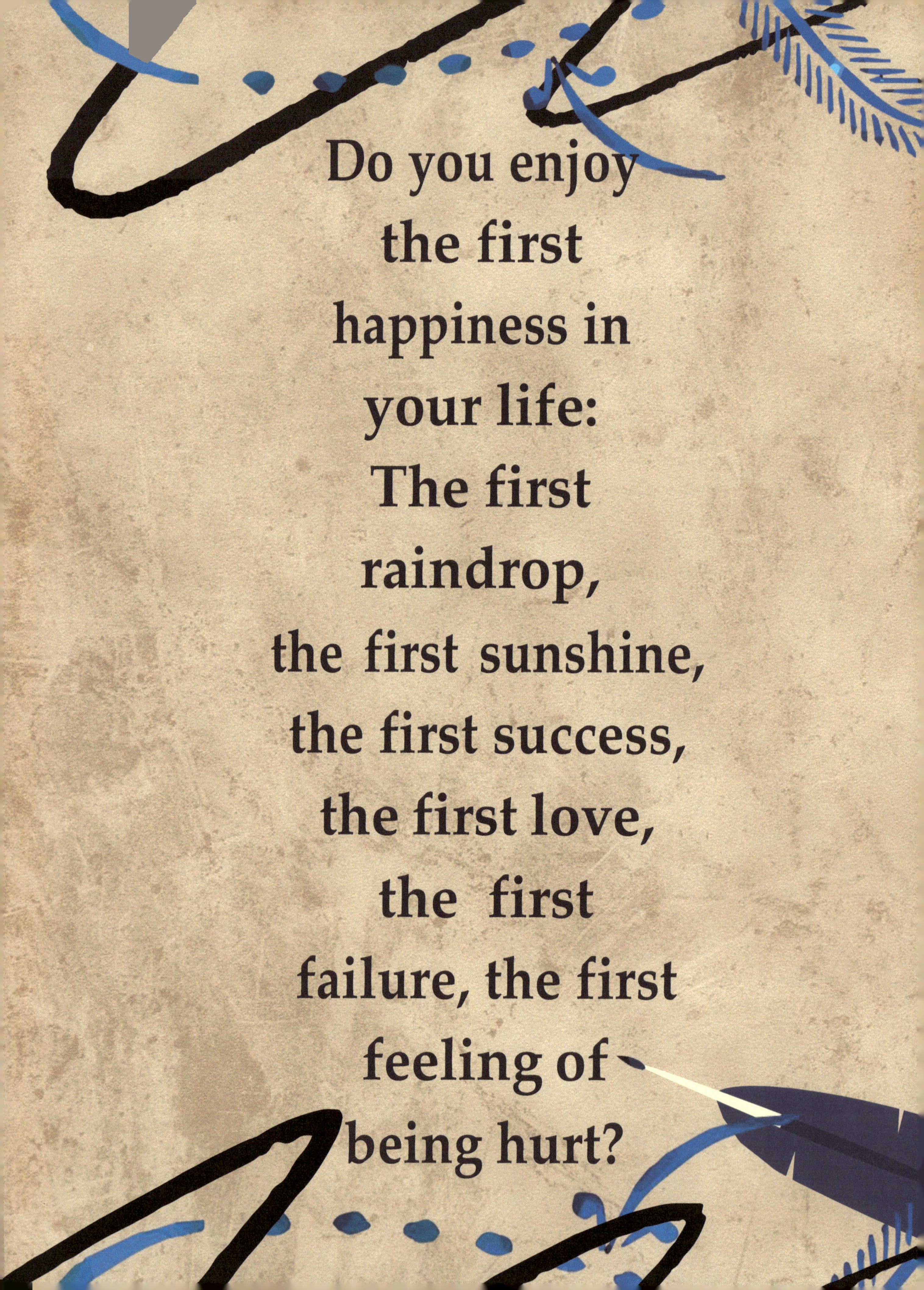
Do you enjoy
the first
happiness in
your life:
The first
raindrop,
the first sunshine,
the first success,
the first love,
the first
failure, the first
feeling of
being hurt?

Adversity and mistakes fortify you for the future

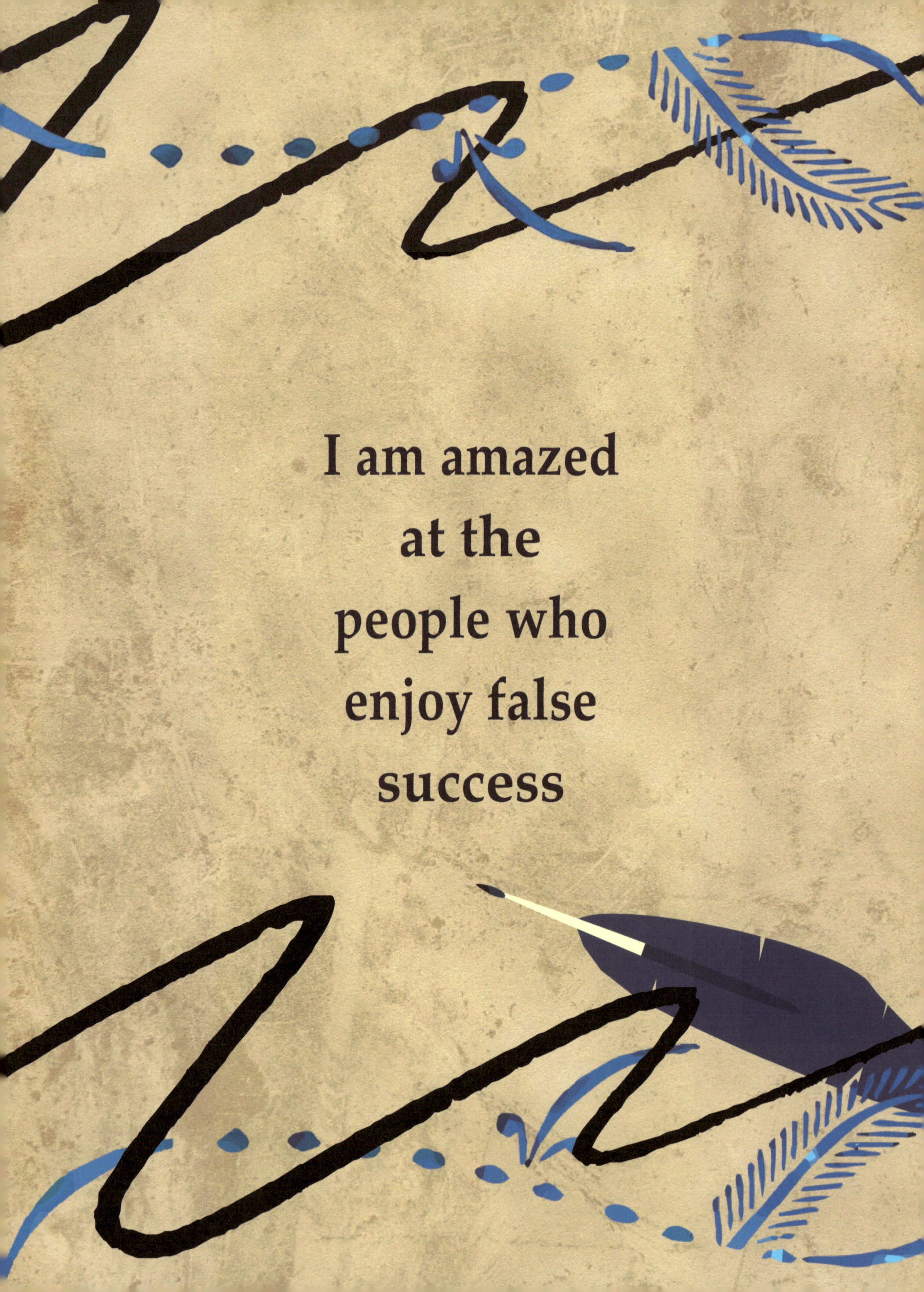

I am amazed
at the
people who
enjoy false
success

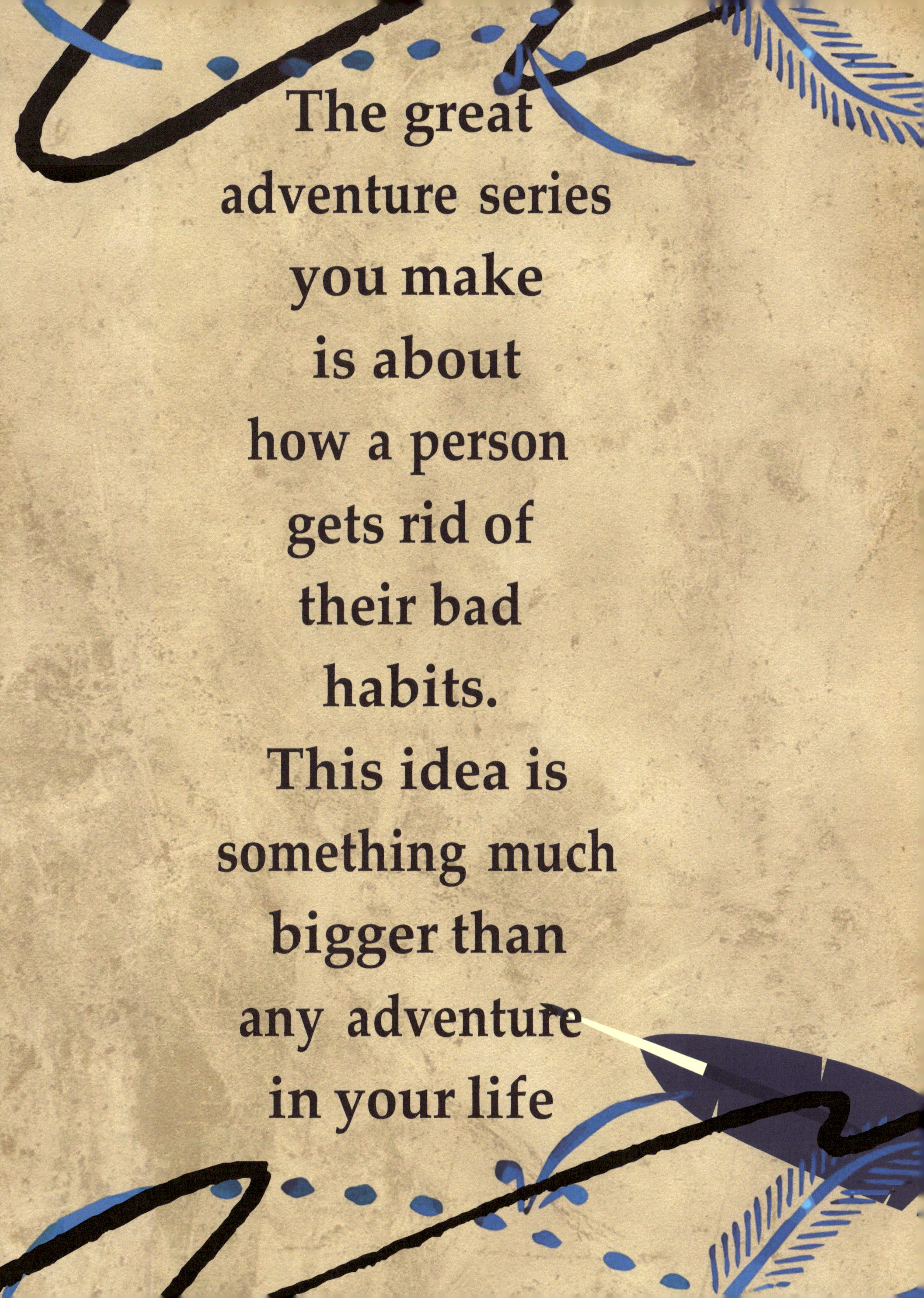

The great
adventure series
you make
is about
how a person
gets rid of
their bad
habits.
This idea is
something much
bigger than
any adventure
in your life

Just always put
a tiny drop
of kindness
to a very
angry person

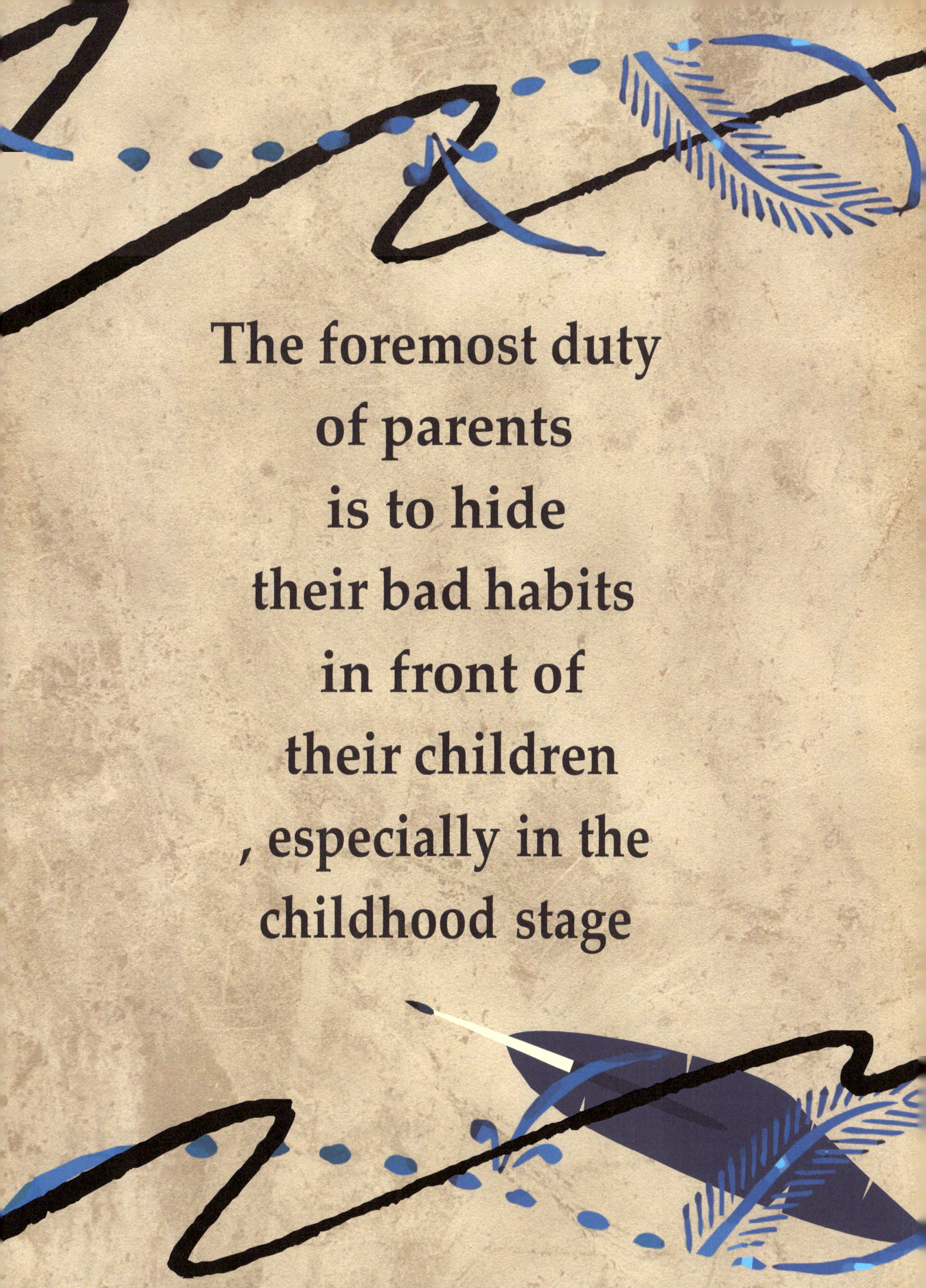

The foremost duty
of parents
is to hide
their bad habits
in front of
their children
, especially in the
childhood stage

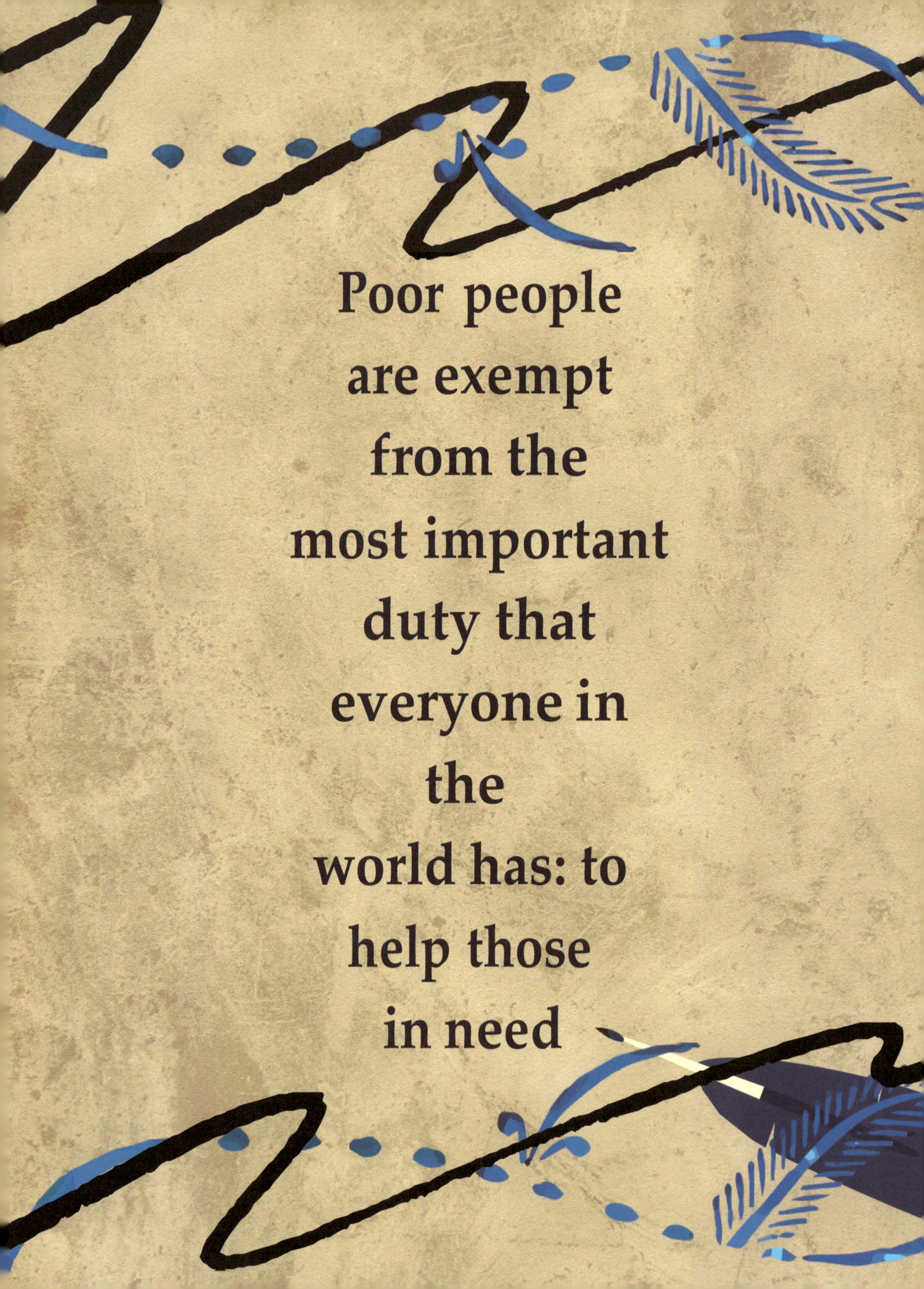
Poor people
are exempt
from the
most important
duty that
everyone in
the
world has: to
help those
in need

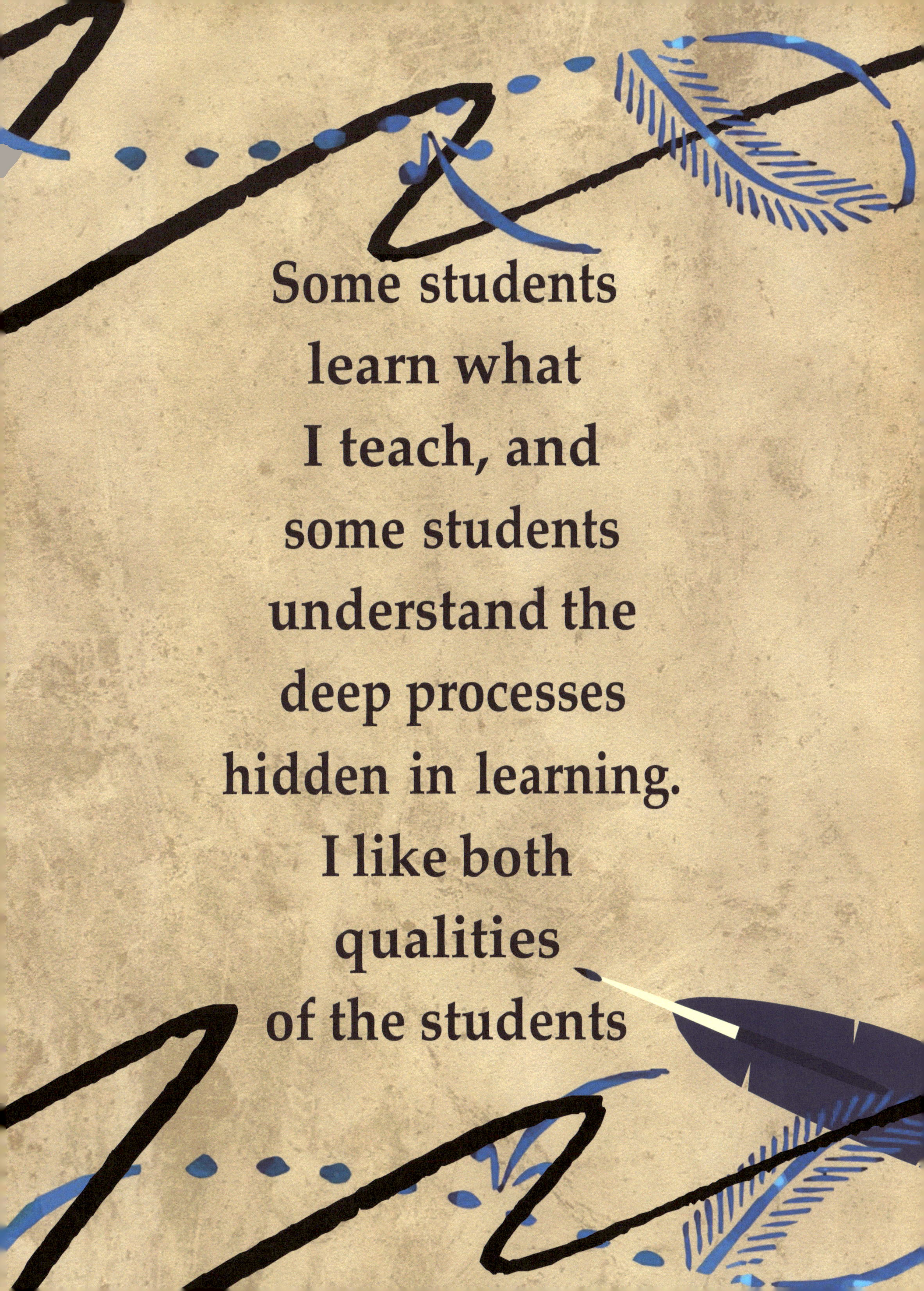
Some students
learn what
I teach, and
some students
understand the
deep processes
hidden in learning.
I like both
qualities
of the students

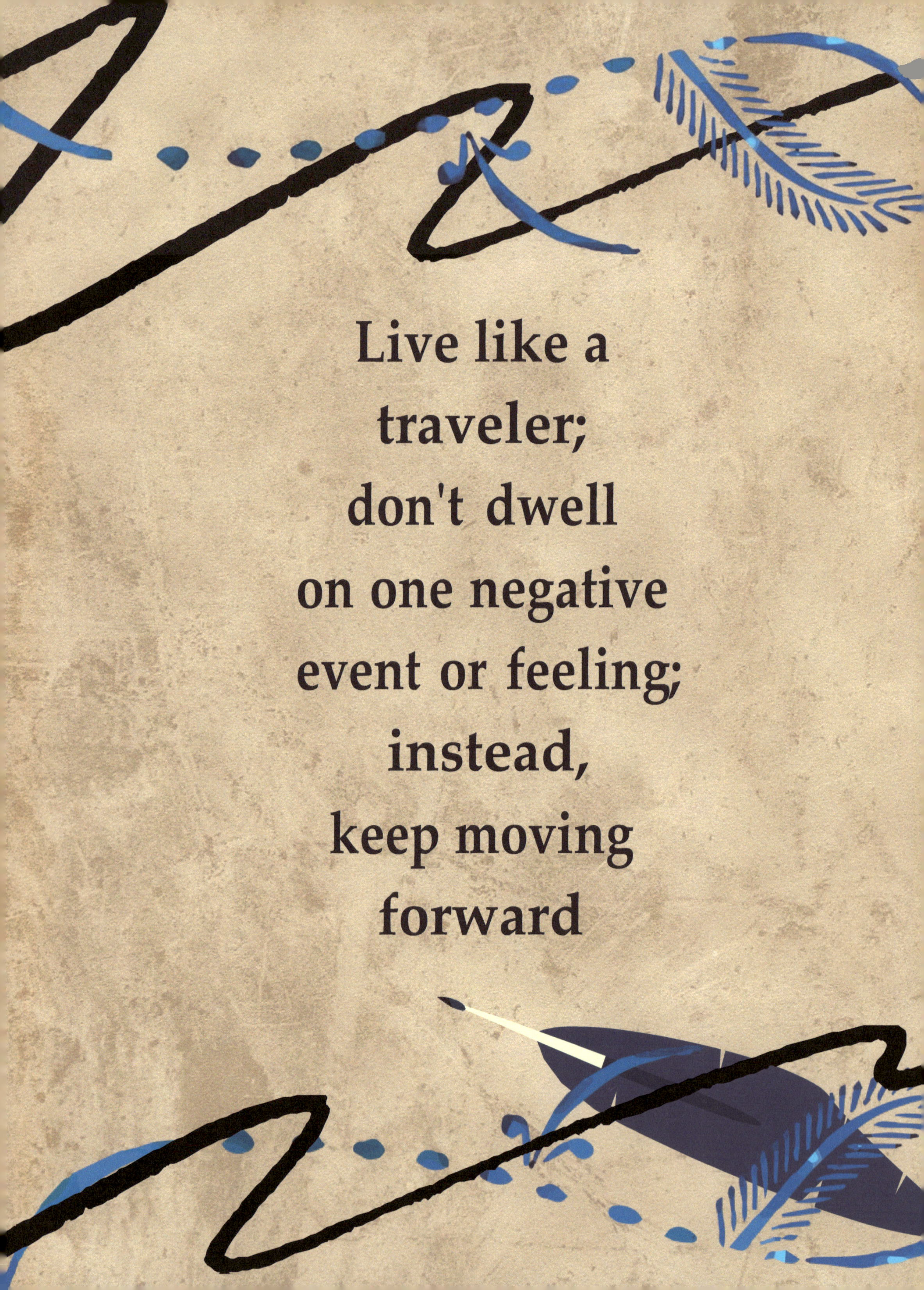
Live like a
traveler;
don't dwell
on one negative
event or feeling;
instead,
keep moving
forward

Inspiration is
the joy you
feel deep inside

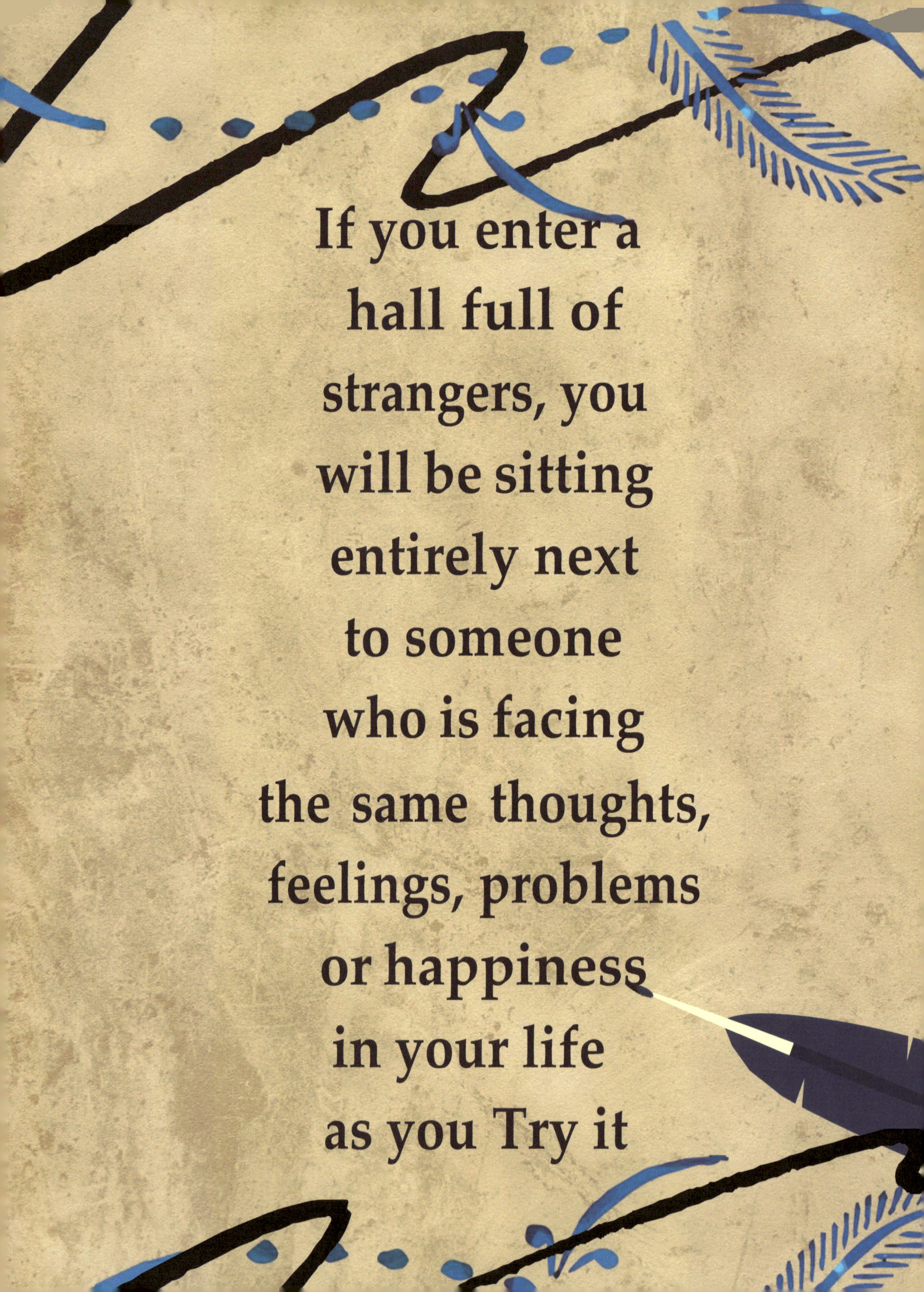

If you enter a
hall full of
strangers, you
will be sitting
entirely next
to someone
who is facing
the same thoughts,
feelings, problems
or happiness
in your life
as you Try it

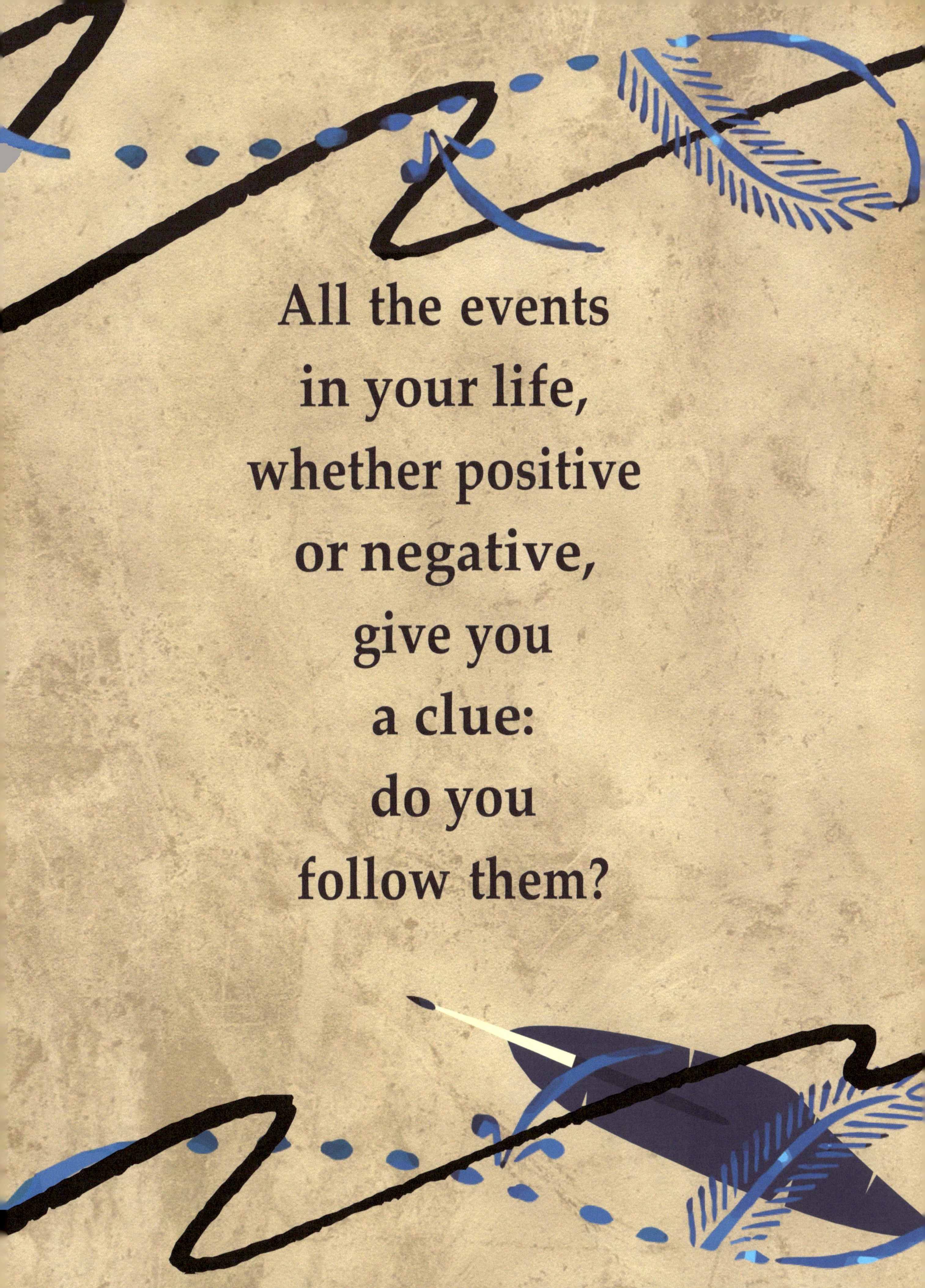

All the events
in your life,
whether positive
or negative,
give you
a clue:
do you
follow them?

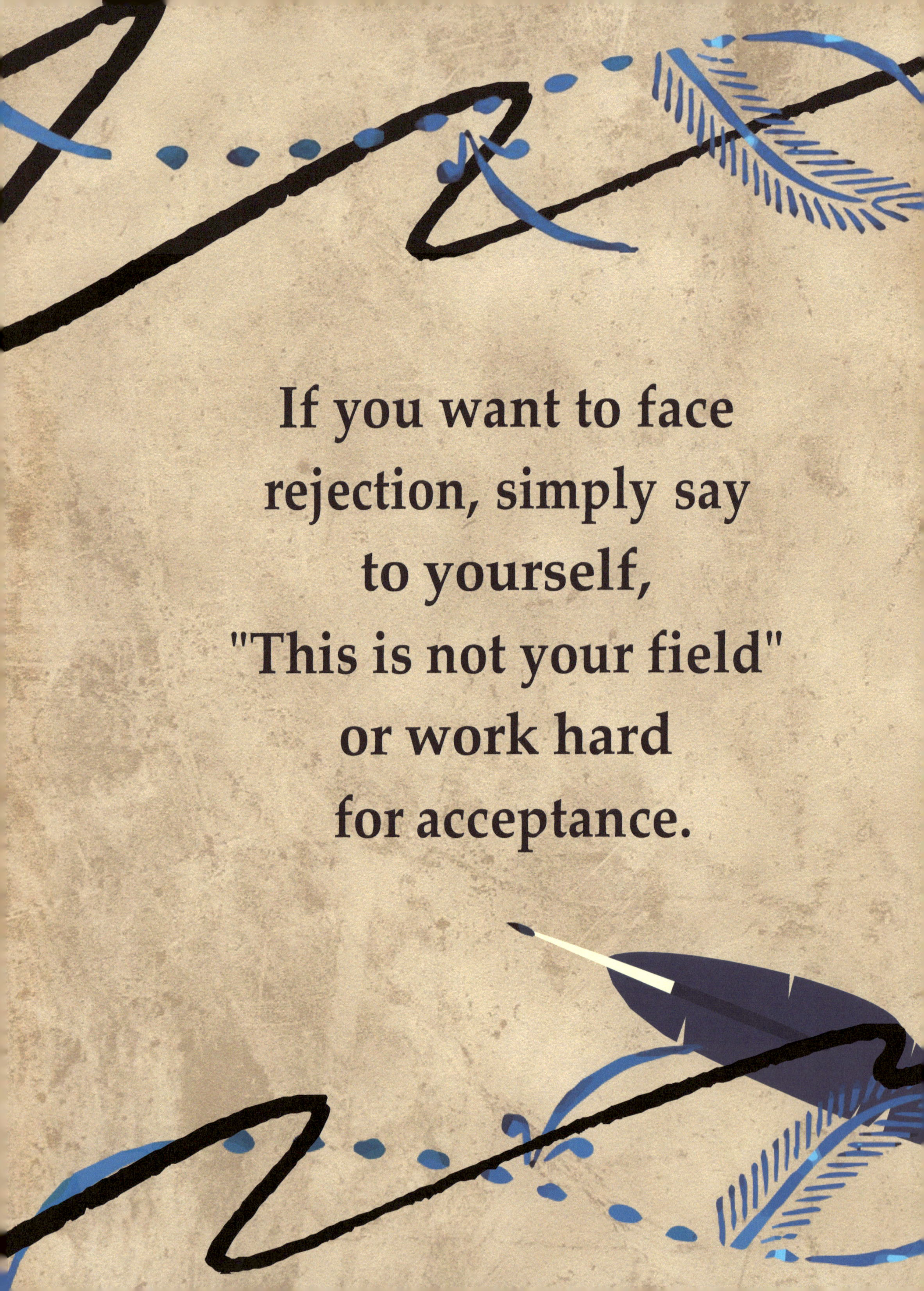

If you want to face
rejection, simply say
to yourself,
"This is not your field"
or work hard
for acceptance.

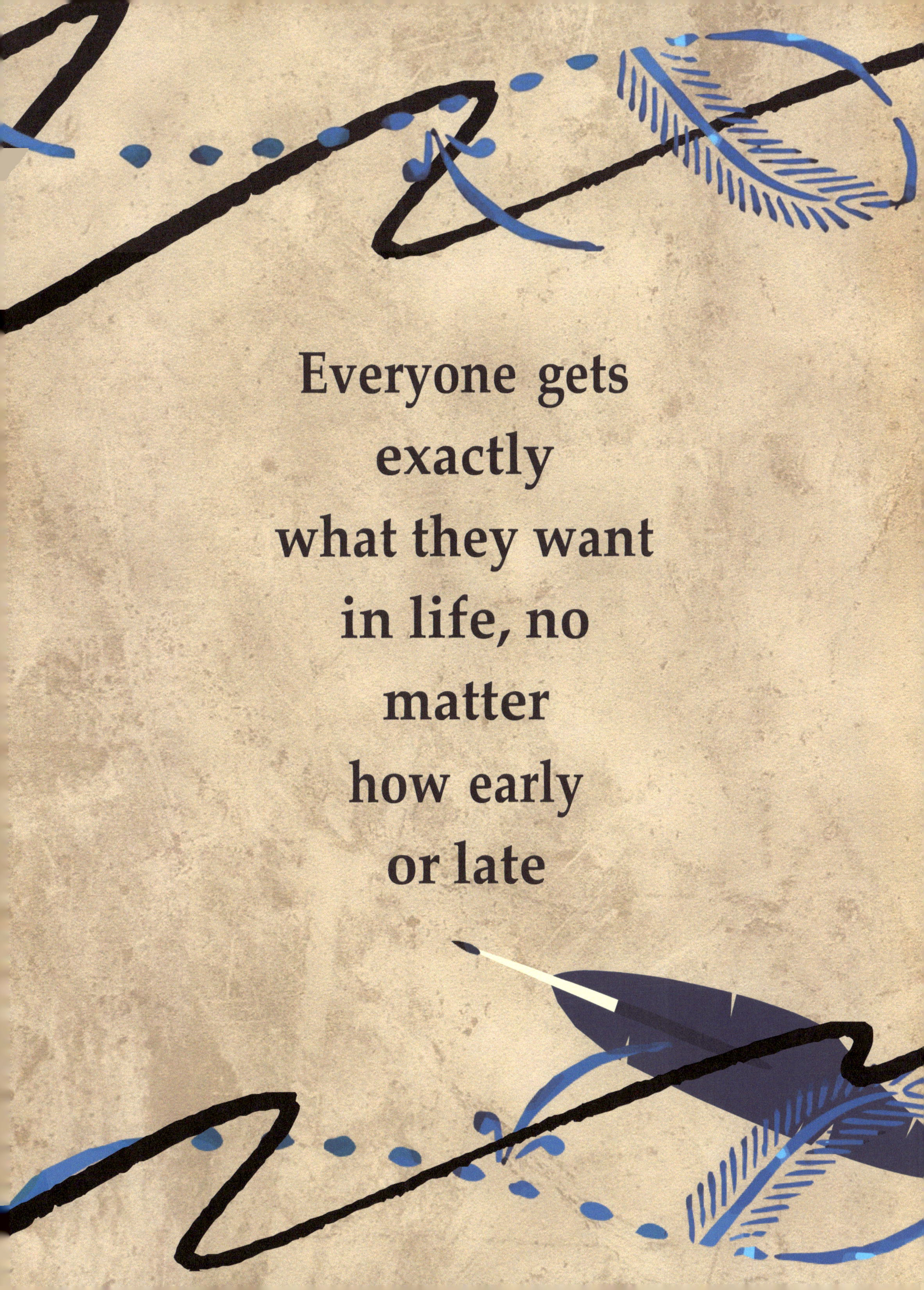

Everyone gets
exactly
what they want
in life, no
matter
how early
or late

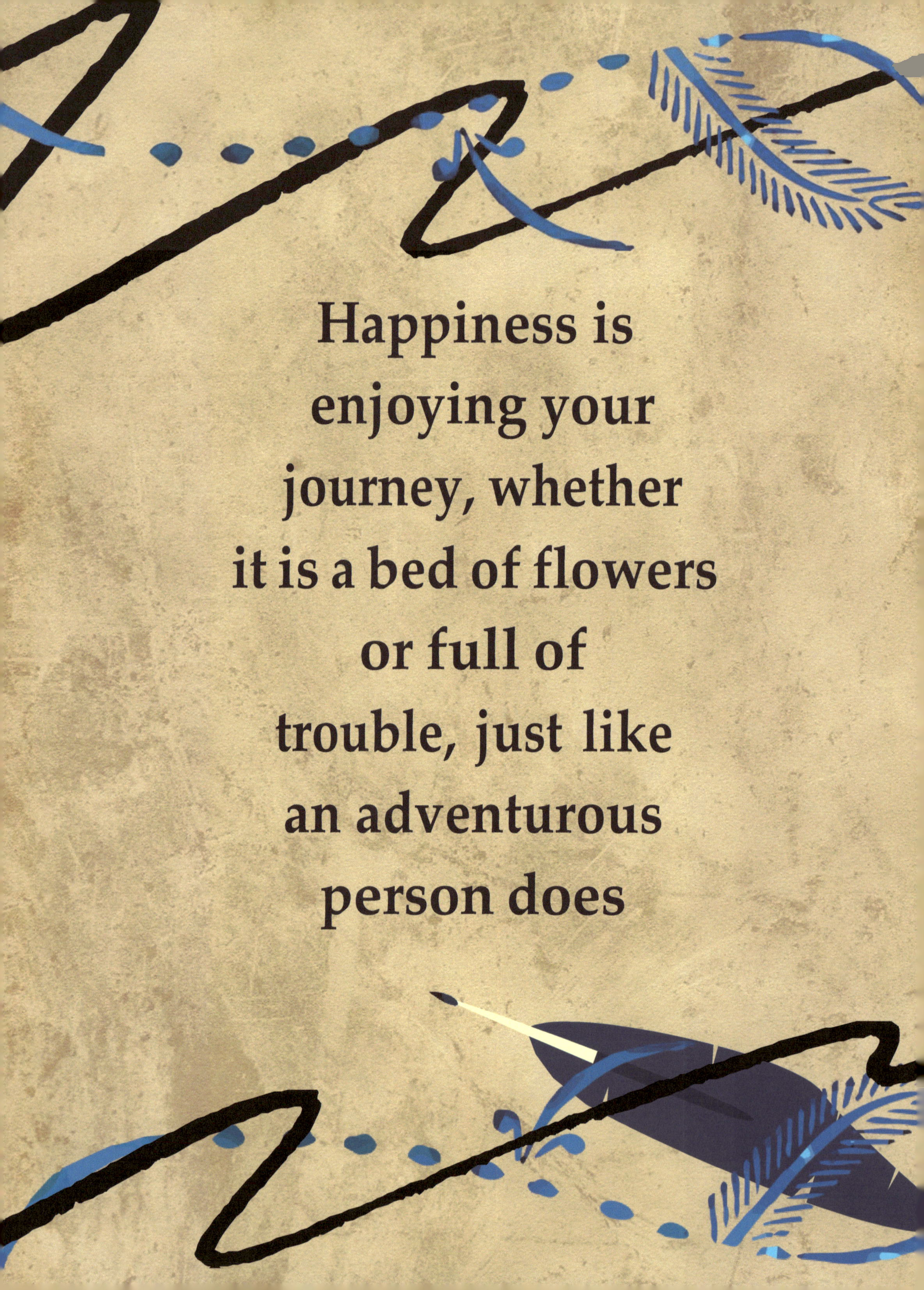

Happiness is
enjoying your
journey, whether
it is a bed of flowers
or full of
trouble, just like
an adventurous
person does

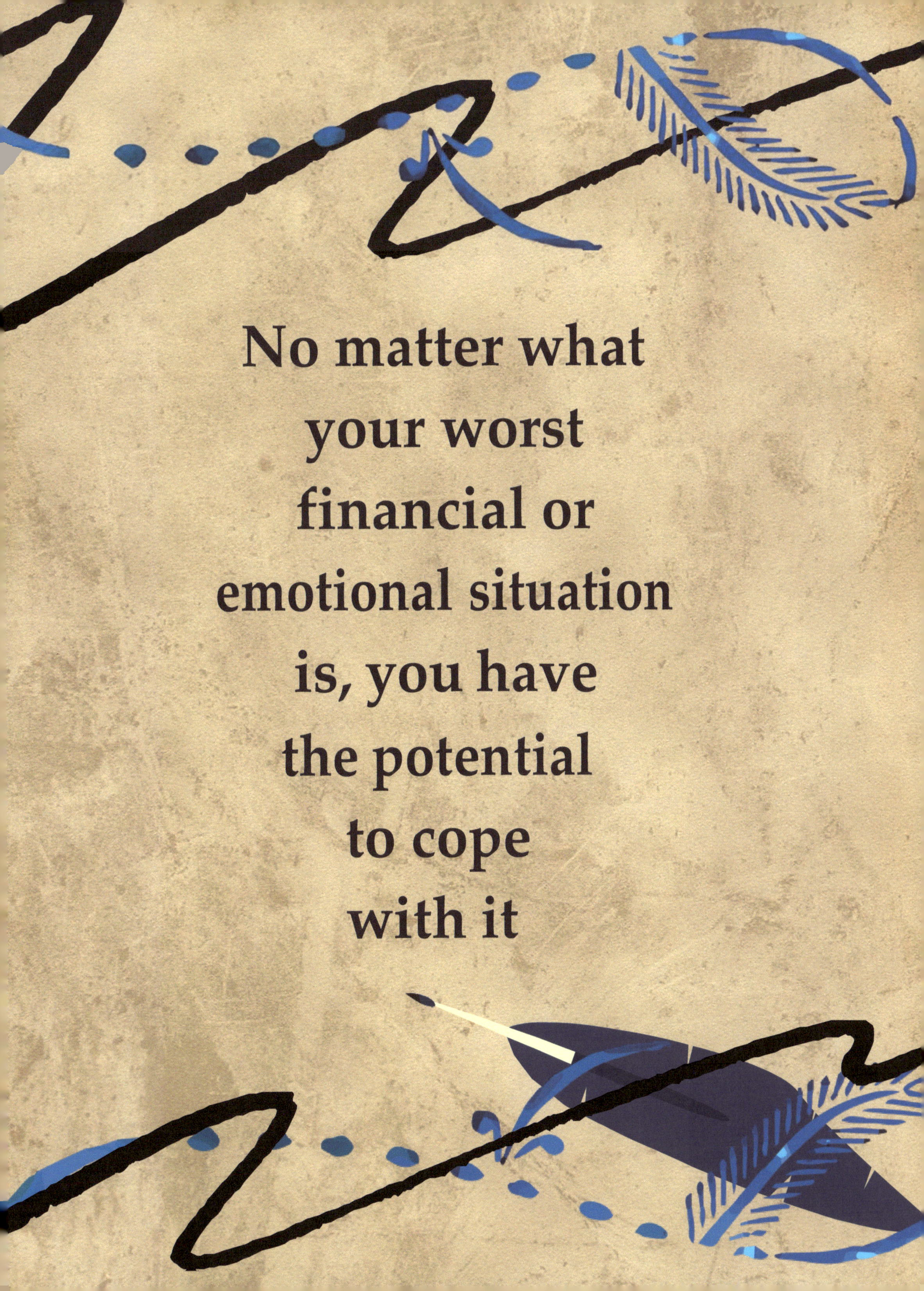

No matter what
your worst
financial or
emotional situation
is, you have
the potential
to cope
with it

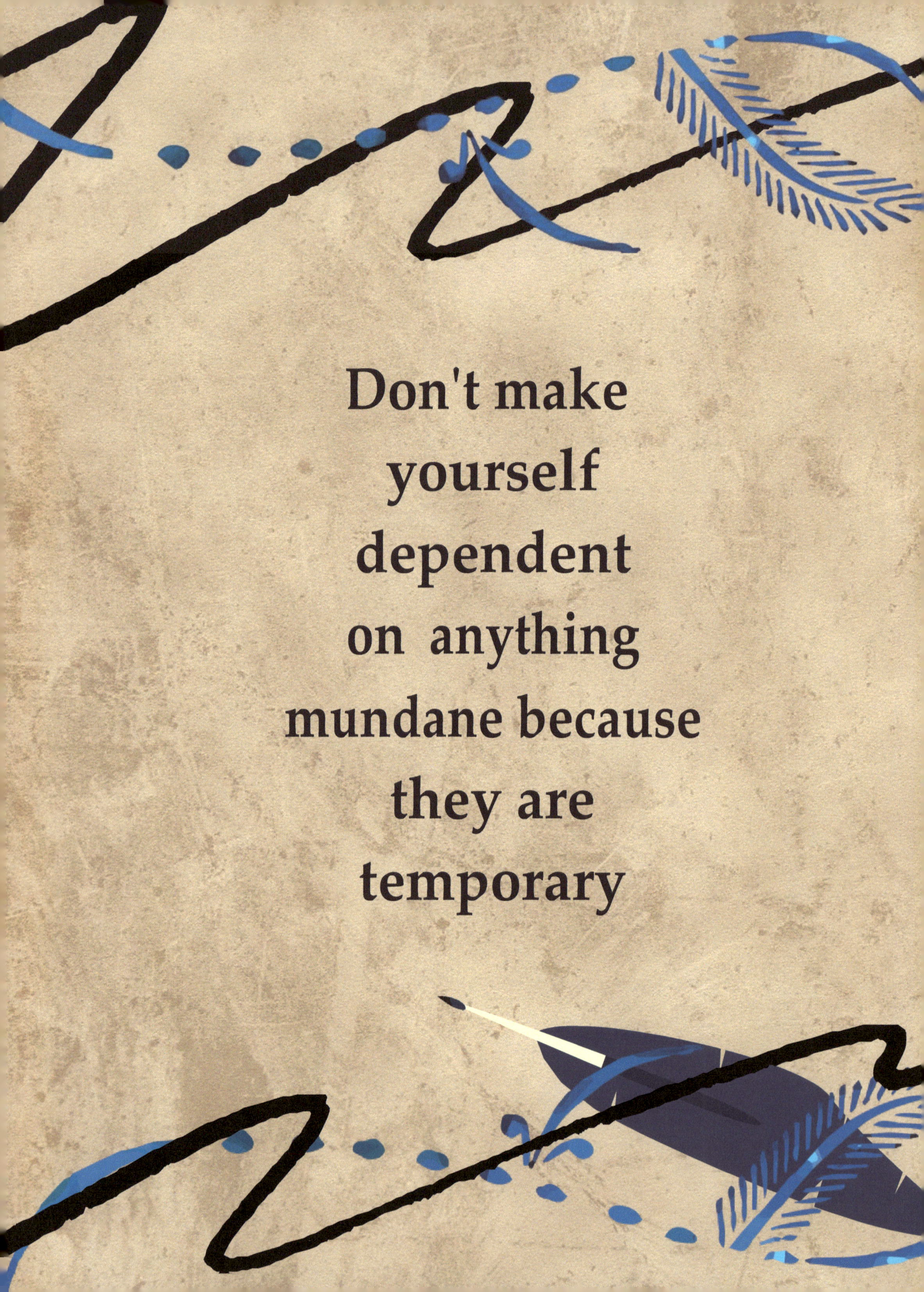

Don't make
yourself
dependent
on anything
mundane because
they are
temporary

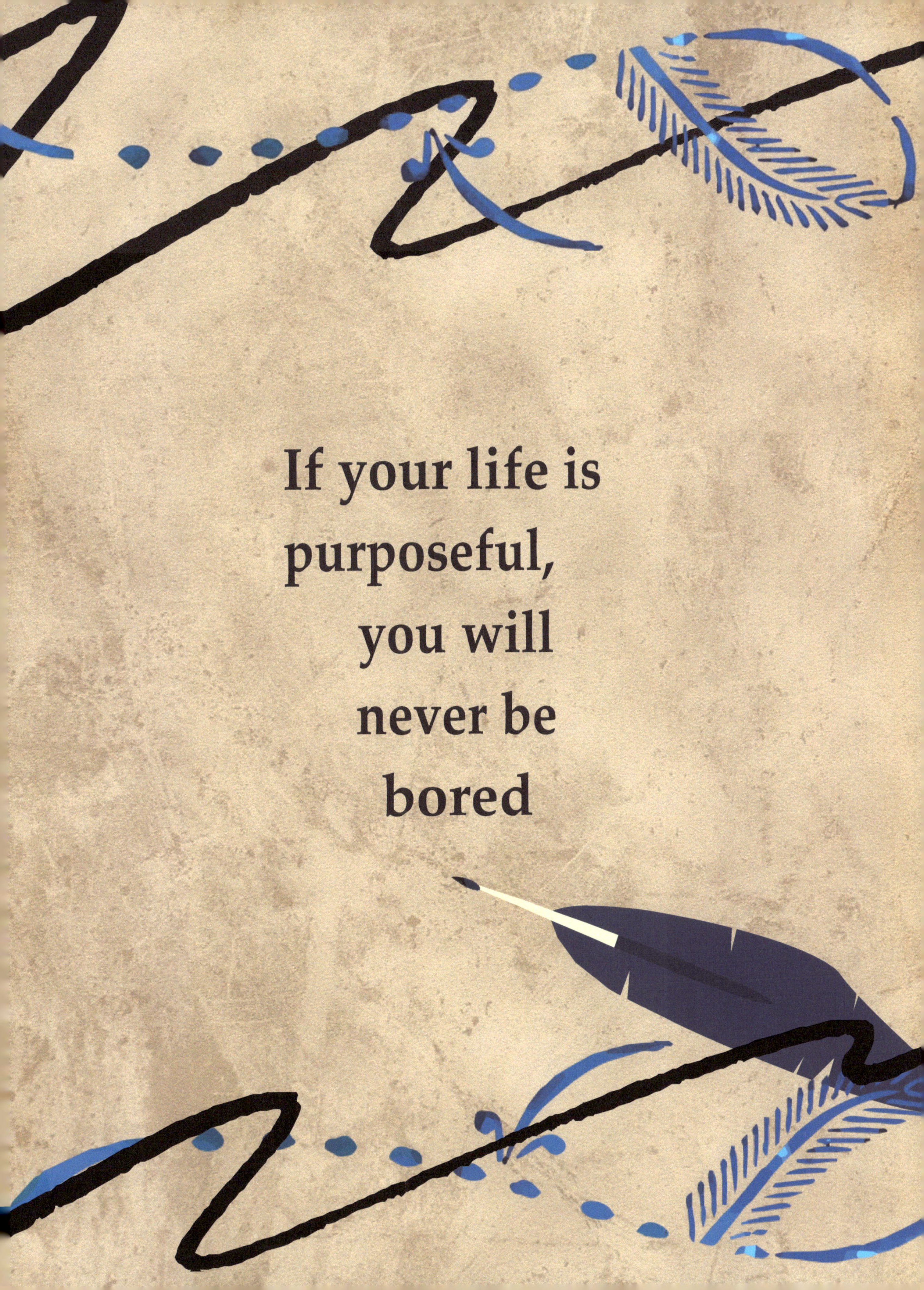
If your life is
purposeful,
you will
never be
bored

Respect the
choices
of others

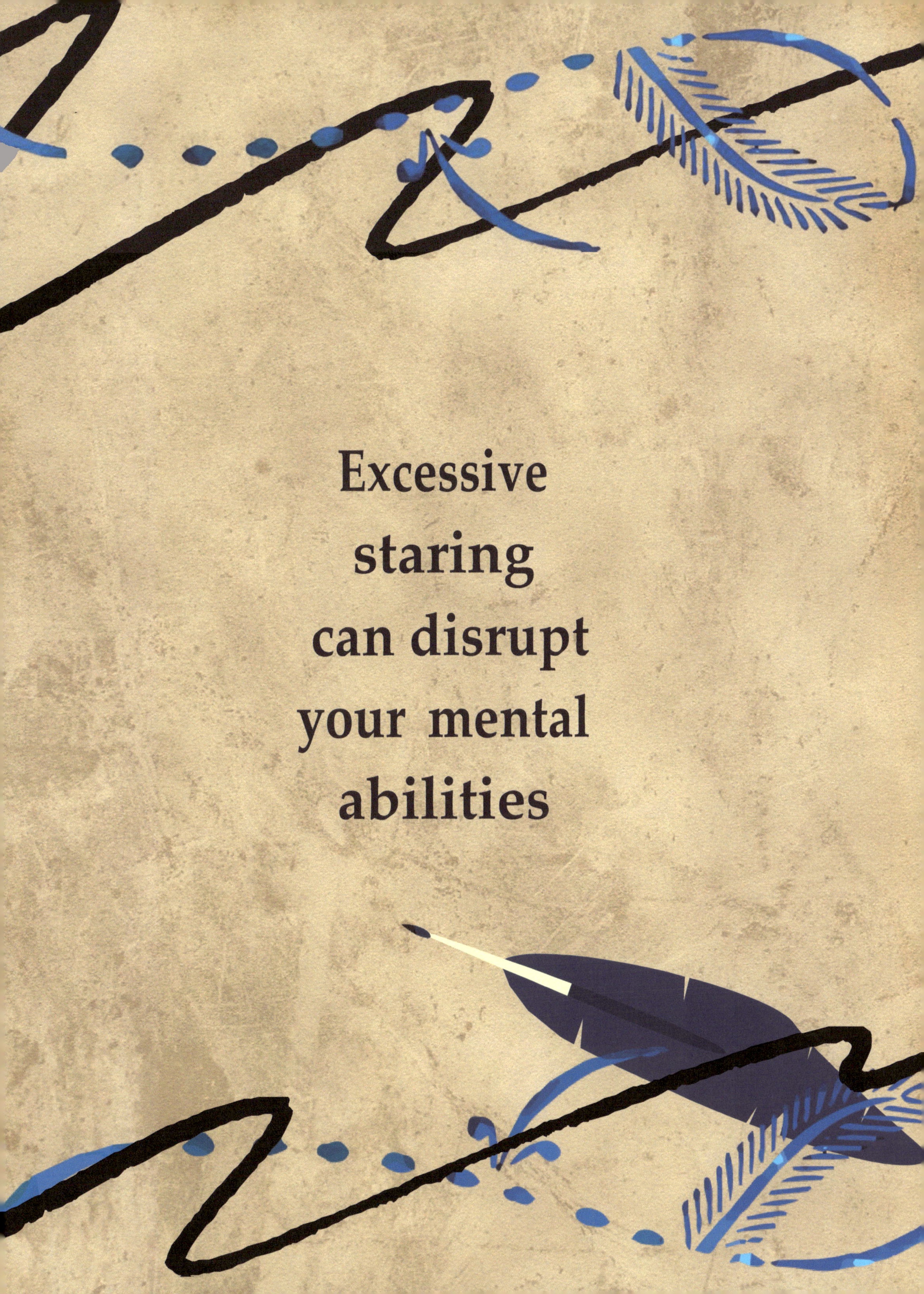

Excessive
staring
can disrupt
your mental
abilities

The more you
love the world,
the more
you feel the
pain of
leaving
the world

Can you get
equal and
honest revenge
from someone?

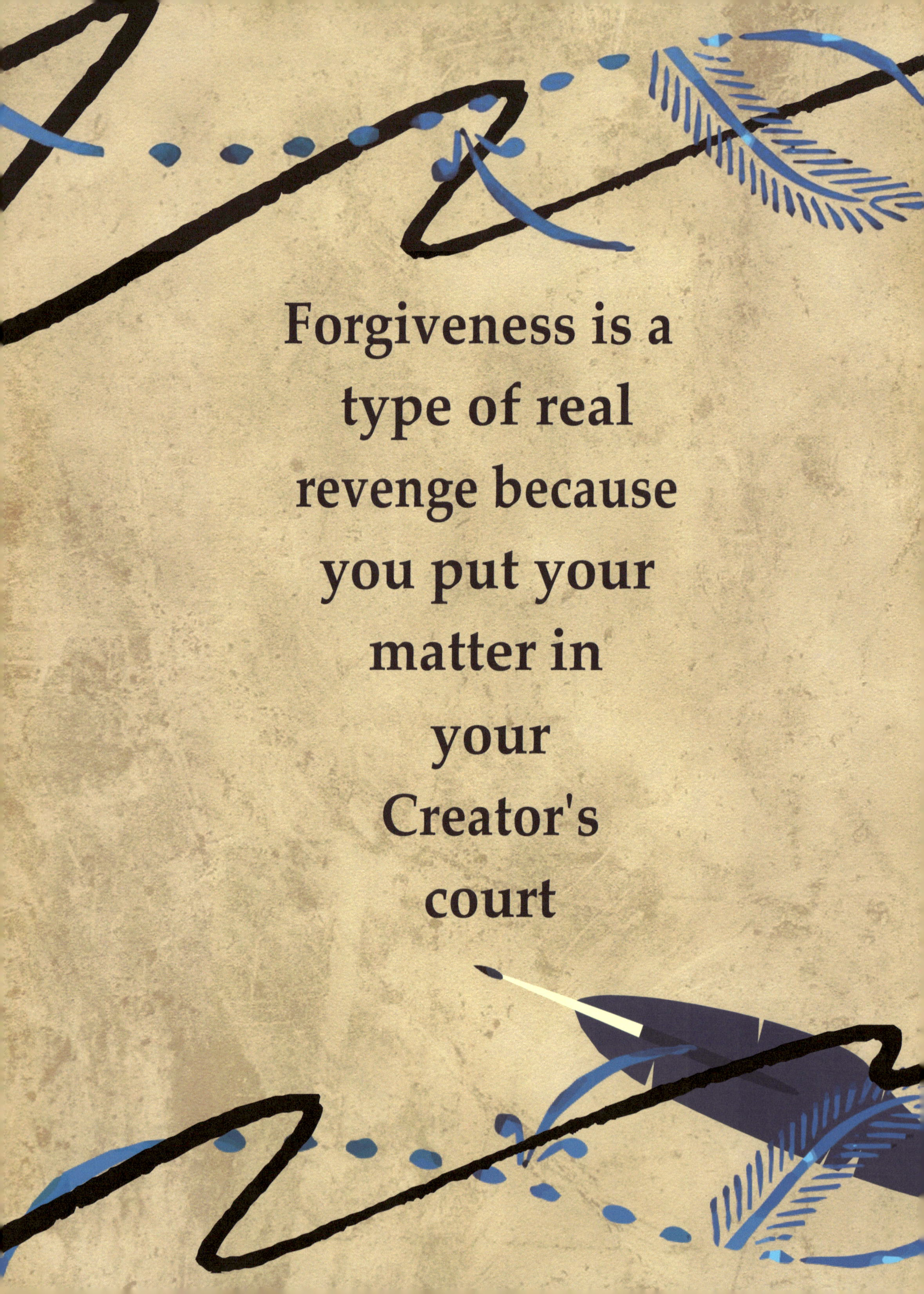

Forgiveness is a type of real revenge because you put your matter in your Creator's court

Focus requires
a love of
your work

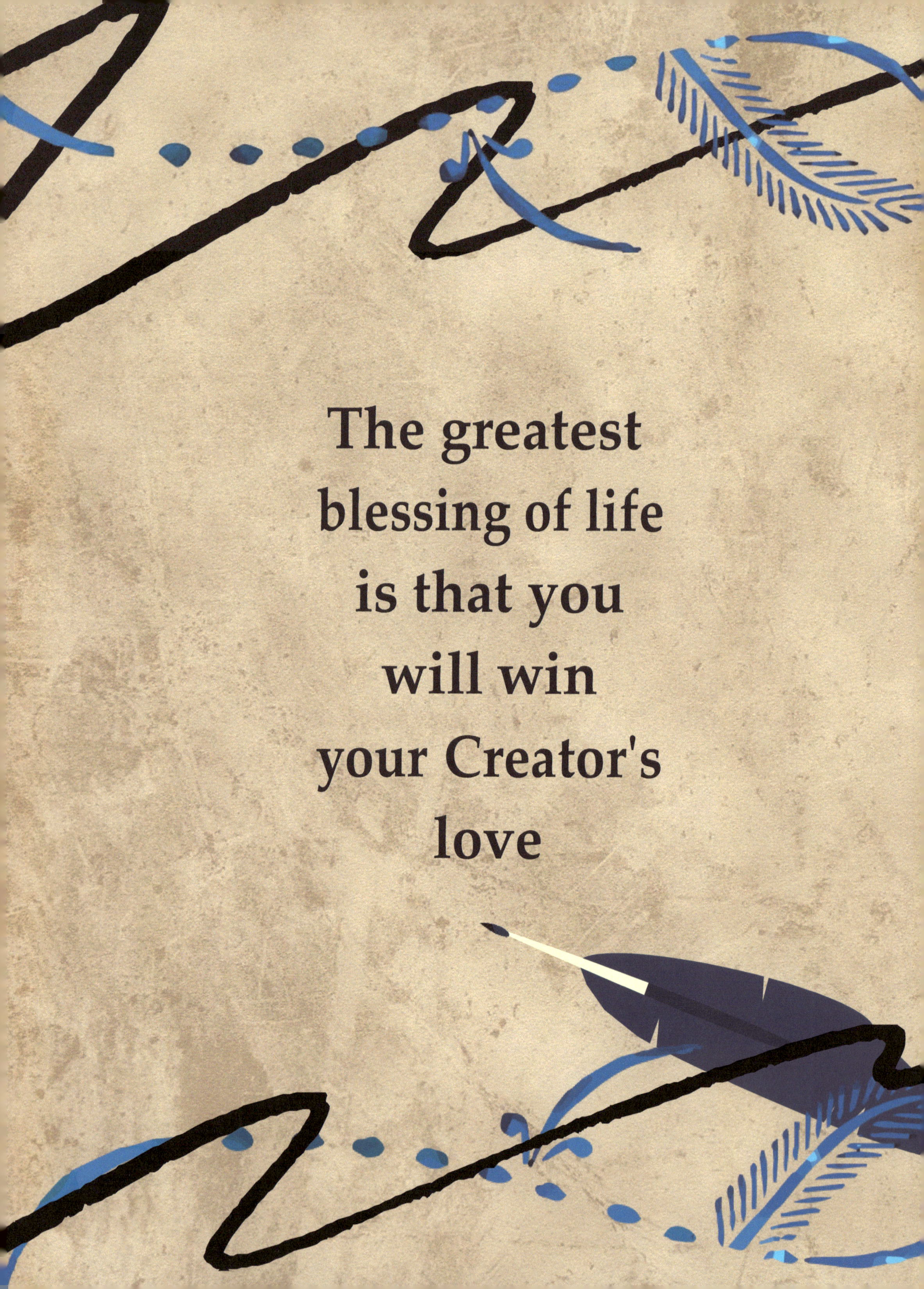

The greatest
blessing of life
is that you
will win
your Creator's
love

Do you praise the management of our Creator?

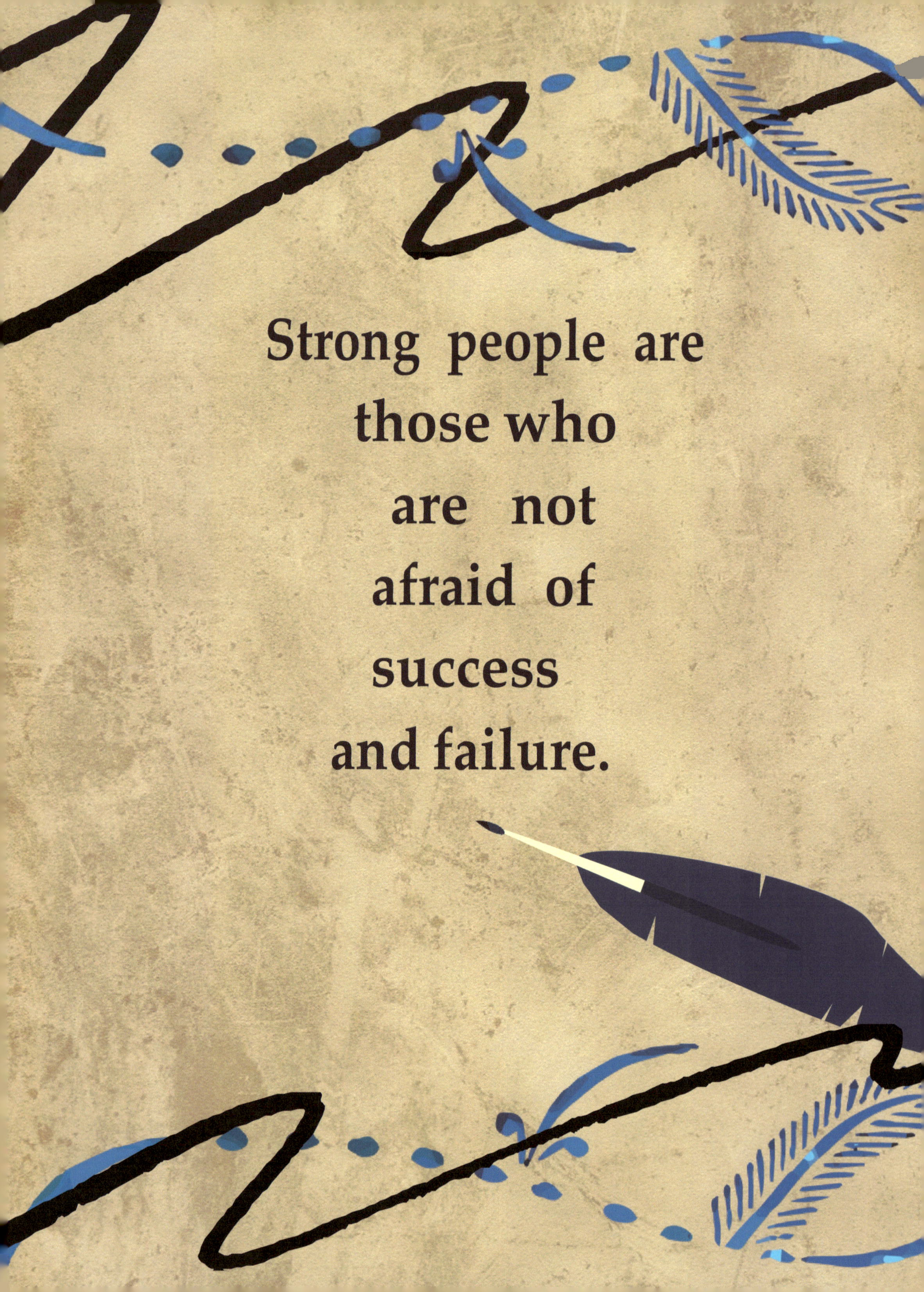
Strong people are
those who
are not
afraid of
success
and failure.